COLLABORATION
IN DEVELOPMENT

COLLABORATION IN DEVELOPMENT

A South African Heritage

Godwin Khosa

AFRICAN
MINDS

Published in 2023 by African Minds
4 Eccleston Place, Somerset West, 7130, Cape Town, South Africa
info@africanminds.org.za | www.africanminds.org.za

The views expressed in this publication are those of the author. When quoting from any
of the chapters, readers are requested to acknowledge the author.

ISBN (paper): 978-1-928502-82-1
eBook edition: 978-1-928502-83-8
ePub edition: 978-1-928502-84-5

Copies of this book are available for free download at: www.africanminds.org.za

ORDERS:
African Minds
Email: info@africanminds.org.za

To order printed books from outside Africa, please contact:
African Books Collective
PO Box 721, Oxford OX1 9EN, UK
Email: orders@africanbookscollective.com

Contents

Acronyms and abbreviations

ANC	African National Congress
ASGISA	Accelerated and Shared Growth Initiative for South Africa
BBBEE	Broad-based Black Economic Empowerment
BLSA	Business Leadership South Africa
GEAR	Growth, Employment and Redistribution
JET	Joint Education Trust
MSA	multiple stakeholder approach
MSN	multiple stakeholder network
MSO	multiple stakeholder organisation
NAPTOSA	National Professional Teachers' Organisation of South Africa
NBI	National Business Initiative
NDP	National Development Plan
NECC	National Education Crisis Committee
NECT	National Education Collaboration Trust
NEDLAC	National Economic Development and Labour Council
NGO	non-governmental organisation
NPC	National Planning Commission
NPO	not-for-profit organisation
NSAGB	National Association of School Governing Bodies
ODA	Official Development Assistance
PPP	public–private partnership
RDP	Reconstruction and Development Programme
SANAC	South African National Aids Council
TMO	temporary multiple organisation
UDF	United Democratic Front

Acknowledgements

I would like to express my sincere gratitude to trustees of the National Education Collaboration Trust who supported the primary study underpinning this book and its publication. I am also extremely grateful to the trustees and my colleagues at the NECT and in the education sector who were part of the interviewees.

A special thanks to my lead supervisor Professor Yusuf Sayed for his constructive guidance and continuously challenging me throughout my studies.

Dedications

To my late parents cum school teachers, Godwin Misabeni and Sarah Mlaleni Khosa to whom I will forever be grateful for teaching me the most elementary, yet important, lessons: how to read, how we should always look for solutions, put in effort and stay the course.

To my wife Dorothy and my three boys – Xirimelo Godwin (3rd), Xihlala and Risana. I relish your endless inspiration.

Preface

This book is a by-product of my PhD studies at the University of Sussex, which focused on modelling a multiple stakeholder approach (MSA) to improving the delivery of education services. I undertook the studies from the mature age of forty-six and a half years, 26 years after I started working as a teacher. Although I produced many written pieces as part of my work, 18 years of no structured academic engagement was too long. I felt the urge to fill my half-empty intellectual glass and to take a breather from management hassles. I was in dire need of some cultural exchange and a new perspective; hence three and a half years of back and forth between Johannesburg and Brighton.

As an adult learner, I logged my study time whenever I opened my laptop or a library book. The PhD on a topic I am passionate about, had worked on for a long time and knew a bit about took me just over 1,200 hours to complete – sometimes doing just 15 minutes a day, sometimes nine hours!

Four motivations inspired me to research and write on the subject of collaboration. The first relates to my professional journey that involved managing several multiple stakeholder initiatives and, in particular, my role in setting up the National Education Collaboration Trust (NECT) leading up to the period of undertaking this research. Between 1996 and 2012, I worked in and with several organisations founded by or involved with multiple organisational networks. These included the Centre for Education Policy Development, the National Business Initiative and JET Education Services, formerly the Joint Education Trust.

Most of my exposure to multiple stakeholder organisations was at JET, a prominent education research and development not-for-profit organisation in South Africa. JET was established in 1992 by 14 major South African companies that provided ZAR 500 million towards restructuring the country's education system.[1] I recall JET's founding chairman, Mike Rosholt, founder and chief executive of a stock-exchange-listed company, Barloworld, and chairman of another not-for-profit organisation, the Urban Foundation, recounting the start of JET as a response to a personal call by Nelson Mandela inviting big business to get involved in fixing the South African education system. More details about multiple stakeholder initiatives in South Africa are discussed in Chapter 1.

Twenty years after the establishment of JET, whilst serving as the chief executive officer, I became involved in establishing the NECT, which was created to address the widely perceived unacceptably poor quality of education. Before the founding of the NECT in 2013, the number of South African learners passing the National Senior Certificate examinations was below 72%, and the number passing with a university entrance certificate was below 25%. Furthermore, international comparative studies in mathematics, science and reading put South Africa at the bottom of the league tables.

The second motivation for undertaking this study was that the MSA is widely used in South Africa to drive political and development initiatives. These initiatives include the development of the anti-apartheid *Freedom Charter,* which involved over 3,000 individuals and organisations; the United Democratic Front (UDF), which was a collaborative formation of political and civil society organisations; the National Education Crisis Committee (NECC), which networked parents, teachers and learners to address education challenges; and government-led programmes such as the South African National Aids Council (SANAC) and Accelerated and Shared Growth Initiative for South Africa (ASGISA). Non-state actors were expected to contribute to both the SANAC and ASGISA programmes (see Chapter 1 for more details). All these initiatives, like the NECT, mobilised and invested significant resources using the MSA, with billions of rands being spent.

The third motivation for the study was to contribute to the theorisation of the MSA, since although repeatedly used in South Africa, it has been used with little scientific basis. I thus sought to characterise the approach and model its operationalisation.

The fourth motivation was to chronicle the application of the MSA in South Africa; it is a historical thread that runs through 60 years and was recently made apparent in the founding of the NECT.

The first and the fourth motivations make for an involved researcher. Whilst it has its disadvantages, being an insider researcher is not a weakness; rather, not being explicit about it and not taking conscious actions to counter its potential bias effects is a weakness. As James Banks maintains, subjective and objective knowledges are interconnected, and making values explicit contributes to the attainment of 'strong objectivity'.[2]

The involvement of values in the case of the NECT extended beyond mine to the 'epistemological community' which included the interviewees, many of whom shared cultural and ideological experiences and interpretations with me. The fact that the respondents were selected from among the active members of the NECT network increased the chances of them sharing some traits, for instance, their affinity for the idea of multiple actor group collaboration. I undertook several steps to strike a balance between what McGregor respectively calls 'theorist' and 'moralist' approaches,[3] where the former works only with analytic ideas and data, and the latter with normative ideas. As Clark proclaimed, I consciously 'sought the truth guided by values'.[4] I promoted openness about my moral and political support of collaboration to improve education and acknowledged most of the respondents' support for the same ideas. I consciously bracketed personal views and identified contradictions that were likely to be a result of interviewees' value-based comments. Data was deliberately subjected to multiple analytic steps. I openly and continuously acknowledged that the research was predicated on a personal commitment to systematically understand the phenomenon of the multiple stakeholder approach.

On the positive end, I used my understanding of the NECT case study and its group cultures, and my rapport with the interviewees, to delve deeper into the subject of the enquiry. At the same time, I took conscious measures to minimise the potential negative impacts of unchecked subjectivity.

The PhD study used a conceptual framework drawn from various theories including network theory, social capital theory and organisation theory, as well as a review of the relevant literature to examine the NECT in South Africa. It is based on a qualitative research approach with primary data collected through in-depth interviews with key stakeholders and members of the NECT including the NECT staff, founding members and the actor groups comprising the state, unions, funders and civil society. This was complemented by a review of relevant documentary data. The data was analysed using a thematic analysis approach to answer the main question concerning the characterisation and operationalisation of the MSA and sub-questions which are: Why have actor groups in education joined the NECT network? How do the actor groups in the NECT network experience their engagement with each other? And how is the NECT network managed by the secretariat?

To uphold the research ethics commitments made, quotations and specific inputs have been delinked from the names of people in most cases.

I hope you enjoy reading the book, which was written to make it easy for any reader from any field to read with ease the academic work that forms the background of the book.

Prologue

Discover and utilise existing indigenous capabilities
before burning energy on building new ones.

When you are in New York, the behaviour of the people you see conforms to the typical image we have of New Yorkers, who are just a fraction of Americans. Most people would be seen clutching their coffees, briskly walking and looking stretched. Americans, both inside and outside America, share an unmistakable sense of being the first nation in the world. The less emotionally diplomatic spell out their identities to your face – we make America great again. The British also display a distinguishable typical common character. In London, they, too, clutch their coffees. They grimace or don't smile at all and mind their own business. They unmistakably see themselves as the great nation – Great Britain, of the commonwealth distinguishable from the entire Europe (at least to the majority that got the Tory government back at 10 Downing Street). The sense of being the greatest among the Americans and the British could be associated with the sense of conglomeration of states or of the kingdom encompassing constituent regions (England, Scotland, Wales and Northern Ireland).

The way of doing things and the levels of confidence from the West is different from that which is expressed by the people from the East. Take the Chinese in their capital Beijing. They clutch their bottles of Chinese tea or water. On the lighter side, they are people who will find a way to work around anything, including using patented intellectual insights and eating anything that moves. Quite resilient people. People with doubt need to visit their markets to see the sorts of roasted insects, reptiles and mammals that hang publicly to entice customers. Other common characteristic behaviours are noticeable in cities such as Mumbai in India. The people shake or twist their heads when they speak. They clutch water bottles, and chew and spit out residues of Paan leaf wrapped around betel nut, quicklime and flavourings. People from the populous China and India would express themselves as the unique people in the world with different solutions to life. They go by with life in their ways without much external control or voluntary mimicking of other nations.

The ways of doing things in the West differ from those in the East. Overall, the latter is more mindful than those the former. The question is: How do people from the South exhibit themselves – for example, South Africans, Kenyans, Zimbabweans and Nigerians? Besides attire and accents, Zimbabweans, Kenyans and Ghanaians are known as nations that have had and relished their independence for much longer. They would be known for the high levels and good quality of education, at least among African countries. South Africans are well known for their struggle against apartheid and the unique reconciliatory independence process, and perhaps for the recent grand state corruption.

The moral of these national stories, which you may dispute, is not about some concrete differences; rather, it is an attempt to identify what South Africans are known for and whether what they are known for is a result of conscious choices of national artefacts that make up the South African identity. So, would South Africans be characterised as a nation 'just struggling along and reconciling at every point of the way? Would South Africans seek to fit in or pursue reconciliation opportunities anywhere and everywhere in the world, as they have in the past, and look for opportunities to trade in their competitive advantages for conciliation? Would this be the way to go when they sit around negotiation tables with forceful people from the West and those from the East content with their own solutions that work, regardless of market principles? What would South Africa export in the realm of philosophy and identity?

A recent example of research investment by the Portuguese into the concept of *ubuntu* is revealing. The Portuguese have, since 2009, been working with some South African counterparts to understand the concept of *ubuntu* and produce a youth training programme, *Ubuntu Youth*. The simple meaning of *ubuntu* is humanity. Its philosophical meaning is the belief in a universal bond of sharing that connects all humanity, often expressed as 'I am because we are'. In its 2022 plans and annual report, the National Education Collaboration Trust confirmed working towards training a million young people in the philosophy of *ubuntu*. In this case, South Africa can be congratulated for collaborating with Portugal. South Africa, with a world-class philosophical heritage, can also be rightfully criticised for reimporting a finished training product whose origins are (South) African.

The message here is that South Africa is under-capitalising on its rich ways of doing business. One such way, the focus of this book, is collaboration. This approach portrays similarities to Nguni culture and philosophies such as *tsima* and *ubuntu*. *Tsima* is an approach where 'families or communities faced with burning challenges get together, lend a hand and address the challenge quickly'.[5] Raymond Suttner likens this national heritage to the humanism which was practiced in Zambia under Dr Kenneth Kaunda and the negritude advanced by Leopold Senghor of Senegal.[6]

The collaboration approach, which has been extensively used in South Africa, should be promoted to the same extent that the Japanese have entrenched and exported their 'small incremental improvement' Kaizen approach. There are many such under-explored indigenous ways of doing business in Africa. For example, how many people know that no one gets robbed at our taxi ranks? Why is this? Another example is the traditional leadership system. A case in point is how an Induna in my village adjudicated an environmental protection hearing. He listened to witnesses and arguments under the prosecution of one of his senior council members and concluded by saying 'Anyone passing Mageva village will know that the system runs without fear or favour, is not based on whether people are related or not; no one will cut down trees so that our children and grandchildren grow up without trees'. What a classic case of good governance from an induna who has not seen the inside of a classroom! Why wouldn't these systems find ways into how we run development and organisational performance initiatives? As the World Bank puts it, where improvement is required, the need is not so much building new capacities as discovering and implementing more strategic and effective utilisation of existing indigenous ones.[7]

The open proponents of indigenous insights such as Chinua Achebe have fought for a place for African stories, voices and knowledge systems. Such a struggle involves influencing global and national networks and systems and, equally importantly, passing indigenous knowledge from one generation to another, in the same way that Chinese people in the mountainous areas carefully pass insights into the complex process of tending rice beds to young generations. Achebe chronicles the need to use, among other methods, storytelling. Storytelling is, by the way, a method that the Harvard Business School has embraced and is exploiting extensively.

There is no need to cringe when African culture is used to inform science. This book uses history, interviews and documentary evidence from South Africa to weave together a story, arguments and lessons about collaboration.

1.

Memoirs of Collaboration in South Africa

Collaboration, specifically the multiple stakeholder approach (MSA), is a common feature in South African history, both before and during the democratic era.

The MSA was used during the apartheid era by non-governmental organisations as a method for driving the development of the non-white populace who suffered inferior public services and political disenfranchisement. Non-governmental structures had to devise innovative ways to provide public services to these neglected groups.[8]

During the apartheid era, multiple stakeholder initiatives comprised compacts, social movements, political initiatives and development organisations. The MSA was used in political and development programmes, and specifically in education improvement, where initiatives were conceived and implemented by anti-apartheid organisations that promoted development inclusive of the neglected black population, including Indians and people of colour, who make up more than 90.6% of the population of the country.[9]

To lay a basis for the discussions that follow, I introduce and define in Box 1 the frequently used concepts in the book in relation to the analysis of MSA in the South Africa context.

Box 1: Meanings of some frequently used concepts

Multiple stakeholder approach (MSA) is understood as a collaboration between non-state actors, and in some cases with the state, to advocate for or to implement development initiatives in general and education interventions in particular.

Network organisation is a construct referring to inter- or multiple-organisational ties among organisations that share a common goal and agree on common investment of resources aimed at achieving that goal. It implies a level of shared governance and authority over common operations.

Multiple stakeholder network (MSN) is an organisational manifestation of the connection of distinguishable actors that share goals. A flow of tangible and intangible resources forms among them.

Multiple stakeholder organisation (MSO) is an organisation that has been set up by multiple independent organisations, referred to in this text as parent organisations (Meer-Kooistra, 2015).[10] An MSO takes the form of a temporary multiple organisation (TMO), with a minimal structure or secretariat responsible for the coordination and technical operations of the MSO. MSOs are distinguishable from single organisations that have common governance and management authority and systems. In MSOs, a manager cannot exercise authority or legitimate organisational power over the actor groups.

Actor group is a concept employed to refer to each of the four categories of both founders of and participants in the case of the NECT network: government, private sector, teacher unions, and civil society. The meanings and delimitations of these actor groups are further explored in various sections of the book.

Collaboration charters and movements

Apartheid-era collaborations comprised political initiatives, education improvement initiatives and organisations. The *Freedom Charter* was one of the first manifestations of the MSA used in the political realm.

A liberation charter, the *Freedom Charter*, was adopted in 1955 by over 3,000 South Africans drawn from several political parties, trade unions, churches and individuals from all walks of life. Suttner maintained that 'the *Freedom Charter* is part of the national heritage, but of a special kind relating to its being part of a "democratic stream".'[11]

The second notable demonstration of an MSA, also in the political realm, is the United Democratic Front (UDF). The UDF is a now-defunct major anti-apartheid network of organisations that emerged in the 1980s from a non-racial coalition of about 400 civic, church, student, worker and other non-state organisations. Established in 1983 in a similar manner to the Freedom Charter, the UDF was an *organisation*, established primarily to fight apartheid. Tom Lodge described the UDF as 'a federation linking a large and heterodox collection of organisations varying in function, size, and popular impact'.[12]

The National Education Crisis Committee (NECC) emerged as the first education MSO in South Africa. It was also political in character, being formed in 1986 with the primary purpose of urging students and teachers to challenge the then system of education from within the schools, and to use knowledge and skills to empower students to fight apartheid. The NECC also intended to manage the crisis arising from students' deprioritising education over the fight for political freedom. The NECC's heritage continues to inform current policies and organisational networks in the education sector, including the National Association of School Governing Bodies (NASGB) and the National Education Collaboration Trust (NECT), the primary case study of this book.

With respect to the NASGB, in 2000, the then school governance official in the Gauteng Department of Education, Lawrence Tsipane, along with the author of this book, were tasked, under the auspices of the Centre for Education Policy Development, with the responsibility of establishing the NASGB. We searched the archives, including personal private libraries of former NECC members. We spent some hours in the home of Terry Tselane, the former NECC secretary, to unearth historical NECC documents. We interviewed former NECC officials and the NECC's attorneys, Cheadle, Thompson and Haysom, and crafted the NASGB constitution based on that of the NECC.

Continuity between the NECC and other recent programmes can also be observed in the case of the NECT, the establishment of which involved two former NECC executive committee members, Angie Motshekga, the three-term Minister of Basic Education, and Professor Irhon Rensburg, the then Vice-Chancellor of the University of Johannesburg and member of the first National Planning Commission. More details about the NECT are provided in latter sections.

Collaboration organisations, policies and programmes

The transitional period into democracy, between 1990 when the African National Congress (ANC) was unbanned and 1994, saw the emergence of several MSOs set up by education stakeholders to improve education in South Africa. The Joint Education Trust, which later became JET Education Services (JET), was formed in 1992 by 14 South African companies that donated over R500 million to the organisation. The companies stipulated that the scheme was to be approved by the ANC and would involve all political parties, civil society organisations and teacher unions.[13] A total of 25 organisations were part of this collaboration.

Another example of an MSO is the National Business Initiative (NBI), a business member-based organisation that was launched in 1995 to support the new democratic government in various

6

programme areas including education, skills development and environmental protection. Both the Joint Education Trust and the NBI were launched by Nelson Mandela, who was arguably the most senior, legitimate leader in the nation at the time. Mandela said of the Joint Education Trust: 'We welcomed the formation of the Joint Education Trust in 1992 ... as a move inspired by patriotism and vision.'

Post-1994, the MSA was evident in national policies, macro-development programmes and plans, and organisations. In fact, the multi-party peace negotiations, dubbed the Convention for a Democratic South Africa (CODESA), can be seen as the MSA in practice, bridging the apartheid and the post-apartheid eras.

One of the post-1994 multiple stakeholder programmes was the Reconstruction and Development Programme (RDP). The RDP was one of the first development initiatives to be introduced by the ANC post-1994. Conceived by the ANC before it became the ruling party, the purpose of the RDP was 'to mobilise all our people and our country's resources toward the final eradication of apartheid and the building of a democratic, non-racial and non-sexist future'.[14] The programme encouraged trade unions, sectoral movements and community-based organisations to develop reconstruction and development programmes, and enter into multiple stakeholder forums to harness the democratic government, private sector, labour and communities in 'people-driven programmes'. The *RDP Policy Framework* described a 'people-driven process' as one that 'is focused on our people's most immediate needs, and it relies, in turn, on their energies to drive the process of meeting these needs'.[15] The RDP presented a continuation of the principles and multiple stakeholder heritage of the *Freedom Charter*. This heritage is partly demonstrated in Nelson Mandela's foreword to the RDP framework, which links the intents of the RDP to the *Freedom Charter*. As per the original intention of the ANC, which became the ruling party, the RDP was adopted by the new democratic government. Various forms of inter-organisational initiatives in support of the RDP were implemented by the government.

Four national development initiatives led by the democratic state that exhibit the MSA in practice are identifiable: (1) the Accelerated and Shared Growth Initiative for South Africa (ASGISA), (2) the South African National AIDS Council (SANAC), (3) the National Economic Development and Labour Council (NEDLAC), and (4) the *National Development Plan 2030* (NDP).

SANAC was founded in 2002 with the objective of bringing together government, civil society and other stakeholders to drive an enhanced country response to the public health challenges of HIV/Aids, tuberculosis and sexually transmitted disease.[16]

ASGISA was introduced in 2006. The growth initiative was designed to address several binding constraints including deficiencies in government's capacity and macro- and micro-economic dynamics.[17] ASGISA was not devised to be implemented by government alone; its success would depend on how widely its implementation was discussed, prepared and monitored.

NEDLAC is the vehicle by which government, labour, business and community organisations seek to cooperate. It was established in 1994 through an Act of Parliament to promote the goals of economic growth and participation in economic decision-making and social equity; seek to reach consensus and conclude agreements on matters pertaining to social and economic policy; consider proposed labour legislation and policies before they are implemented or introduced in Parliament; and encourage and promote the formulation of co-ordinated policy on social and economic matters.[18]

The NDP, adopted in August 2012, was one of the last national development initiatives to be adopted post-1994. This macro-development plan presents analyses, visions and a wide range of improvement proposals in transversal functions such as policy-making and promotion of global competitiveness. It focuses on the critical public service and economic development sectors including education, the environment, social development and energy.[19]

Similar to the preceding plans, the NDP emphasises collaboration between government, the private sector and civil society in pursuance of a development vision with targets for 2030.

The NDP is a product of a two-year process of diagnosing the development challenges in South Africa. The diagnostic process and the subsequent development of the plan were overseen by a 24-member National Planning Commission (NPC) appointed by the president in May 2010. The NPC comprised experts representing critical sectors of the economy and was chaired by the Minister of Planning in the Presidency, Mr Trevor Manuel. The deputy chairman was Cyril Ramaphosa, the then Deputy President of the ruling ANC, who became the president of South Africa in 2018.

Trevor Manuel has an interesting history in South Africa's development landscape. Emerging from the 'Cape coloured' community, with a stint in engineering and law, Manuel was one of the cabinet ministers' who served under three presidents – Nelson Mandela, Thabo Mbeki and Jacob Zuma. He boasts being the only cabinet minister to have resigned, only to be re-appointed. He was either a real asset or played his political game well. Or both. Manuel is the father of two macro-development pieces adopted within a period of 16 years: The 1996 *Growth, Employment, and Redistribution* (GEAR) five-year plan, abhorred by trade unions and the Communist Party. GEAR focused on privatisation and the removal of exchange controls. He also drafted the 2012 NDP.

It can be argued that, decades after its adoption, the GEAR principles still underpin much of South Africa's economic policy. Tarnished former President Jacob Zuma narrated that he called Manuel in 2009 and asked him to coordinate the development of a development programme for South Africa. After three weeks, Manuel came back with a plan, and Zuma reportedly said that he was not looking for Manuel's plan but for a plan for South Africa by South Africans. The short story is that Manuel gave it his best shot the second time around, working with a 14-member NPC, and a plan, the NDP, that presents a confluence of the political, economic and cultural ambitions of all South Africans, emerged. The unfolding of the NDP hinged on active citizenry working together – collaboration.

The NPC commissioned papers and invited contributions from the public and various state departments which were used to develop the NDP. The NPC's launch statement asserted that

> South Africa needs well-researched, evidence-based input into policy processes that have long-term economic, social and political implications for development … The commission is expected to put forward research on key cross-cutting, multi-sectoral issues and to produce research reports and discussion papers that provide sound evidence and clear recommendations to government.[20]

The NDP calls for actions that will lead to raising employment through faster economic growth, improved quality of education, skills development and innovation, building the capability of the state to play a developmental, transformative role and creating an active citizenry.

Of the 15 chapters of the NDP, Chapter 9 is dedicated to 'Improving Education, Training and Innovation'.[21] The chapter focuses on early childhood development, basic education, vocational education and training, and higher education (and research). The NDP suggests that education is in crisis and requires an increase in the pace of delivery and the quality of education services, including the removal of binding constraints. The constraints and challenges identified in the education chapter include: sub-optimum education resourcing; poor relationships and coordination among stakeholders; unsuitable human capital to drive the operations of the education system;

weak accountability; and the need to anticipate 21st century educational needs.

The chapter proposes a range of policy and programmatic change instruments. The policy levers include: changing the schooling structure to improve the career paths and efficiency of the flow of students; avoiding further curriculum reforms which burden teachers; human resource provisions relating to the recruitment of teachers and principals, as well as their performance incentives; and the resourcing of schools. The programmatic proposals include: reprioritisation of the focus on education improvement and improvement initiatives; building the requisite skills in schools and districts; organisational culture and relationship changes; and collaborations among stakeholders. A specific proposal that promotes collaboration in education is that for establishing 'a national initiative involving all stakeholders to drive efforts to improve learning outcomes in schools, starting with the worst performers'.[22] This proposal provided the basis for establishing the NECT.

Observables

The MSA-driven compacts and macro-level policies, plans and programmes adopted before and after 1994 present a unique but consistent national approach to responding to societal and development challenges in South Africa. An analysis of these initiatives suggests that development and the delivery of public services are political affairs that require active involvement of and resourcing by more than just the state. The modus operandi of the initiatives involves mobilising sectors, organisations and individuals in society to support or resource collective actions for addressing perceived challenges. This approach portrays similarities to Nguni culture and philosophies such as '*tsima*' and '*ubuntu*', as mentioned in the introduction. *Tsima* is an approach where 'families or communities faced with burning challenges get together, lend a hand and address the challenge quickly'.

The simple meaning of *'ubuntu'* is humanity. Its philosophical meaning is the belief in a universal bond of sharing that connects all humanity, often expressed as 'I am because we are'.

Some common characterisations of the MSA in practice in South Africa are as follows:

- The MSA has been a continuing phenomenon across South African political epochs. It was part of the development and public service improvement discourse in South Africa, before and after the coming into being of a legitimate state. The MSA was used both as an alternative and a mainstream approach to state operations in the two respective periods.

- At the centre of the MSA initiatives is networking and mobilisation of various players or a 'heterodox collection of organisations'.[23]

- MSOs have had recognisable leadership such as President Mandela in the case of the RDP, the Joint Education Trust and the NBI, a senior cabinet minister in the case of GEAR, a senior cabinet minister and a respected former unionist and businessman (would be President, Cyril Ramaphosa) and the Deputy-President (Phumzile-Mlambo Ngcuka) in the case of ASGISA and SANAC.

- MSNs were coordinated by a dedicated secretariat or organisations that served as the engine that propelled the network in pursuance of its visions and ideals. The NECC, SANAC and JET are cases in point.

2.

What Motivates People to Start Collaborations?

New Organisations are Products of Healthy Social Convulsions

B y its ninth year of existence, the NECT had established an extensive web of relationships running into hundreds of organisations. These comprised banks, business associations, teacher unions, non-governmental organisations (NGOs), education departments, retail stores and the labour bargaining council. It had mobilised 1,430 experts and practitioners to get involved in the work of the NECT and supported all nine provinces, all education districts, two-thirds of the in-district specialists, over 110,000 teachers and their managers. Between July 2013 and December 2022, the NECT stakeholder network had raised and invested over ZAR 2 billion in education initiatives. The question that arises from this approach is: 'What leads people and organisations to establish communitarian networks that pool resources and support social development in this manner?' The answer goes beyond the mere existence of social capital and trust touted in the literature, and it is more detailed than only being a part of the national heritage.

Starting an organisation is equivalent to a disruption of existing social arrangements, a result of continuous social convulsions.[24] Social structure, potential benefits, patterns of trust, mobility of resources and the distribution of power in society are long-standing outputs of research into the factors and variables underlying the initiation of organisations. In my own research,[25]

I identified 37 reasons that the four actor groups of the NECT – state, labour, business and civil society – considered. These can be condensed into the eight reasons discussed below.

Eight motivations for setting up an MSA

Crises as a motivation for collaboration

Crises in society are a motivation for actor groups to work together towards establishing collaborations or network organisations. The perceived poor quality of educational outcomes and less than harmonious relationships between the state and other actor groups, were two crises that formed the basis for establishing the NECT. The representative of the business formation expressed the view that education was probably the worst affected by apartheid. Although the National Senior Certificate (school-leaving certificate) results gradually improved from 68% in 2010 to 78% in 2018, only 34% passed with university entrance grades,[26] and the proportion of university entry passes was below 25% in 2012. Five years into the implementation of the NDP, the number of high school graduates eligible to study for science, technology, engineering and mathematics (STEM) related careers was equivalent to 20% of the NDP target of 450,000 for 2030. The 2016 Progress in International Reading Literacy Study (PIRLS) indicated that 78% of Grade 5 learners could not read on their own and understand basic texts.[27] Concern of South Africans about the quality of education has understandably been palpable. The NDP acknowledges that education is in crisis, and the media has largely conveyed a negative critique of education since the dawn of democracy.

Regarding the crisis in relationships, the teacher unions have largely been perceived as the cause of poor relationships in education. The teacher unions themselves conceded this when they pointed to the poor relationship between themselves and the state as the reason for their engagement in the NECT network. The National Professional Teachers' Organisation of South Africa

(NAPTOSA) representative described their historic relationship with the state prior to the establishment of the NECT as a 'cat and dog game' and suggested that the establishment of the NECT had narrowed the gap and normalised the relationship in order to limit the disruptions of the education system. In response to this 'crisis relationship', the South African Democratic Teachers' Union (SADTU), more radical compared to the others, called for the transformation of the relationship with the state in the interest of professional development and the 'transformation of humanity' to 'address challenges of unemployment, poverty and underdevelopment'. The private sector has called for the promotion of sustainable development which engenders inclusive growth imperatives, and the NDP also articulates the crisis in its suggestion that the 'The South African education system needs urgent action'.[28] Similarly, the Minister of Basic Education expressed the need for a collaborative education improvement intervention in her 2015 budget vote speech, referring to the establishment of the NECT in response to the NDP as a result of 'sectoral partnerships', which are working at 'generating improvement for sustainable, scalable application in the sector'.[29] What is clear is that all the actor groups want to see improvements in the education system.

The response to the perceived crisis appears to have engendered a new approach to development challenges: an altruistic, collaborative approach, which is elaborated below in relation to how the private sector worldwide has been reconsidering the way of doing business; where, following the recent global financial crisis, the private sector now speaks a different language, having changed their commitment to *shareholder* supremacy to a commitment to *stakeholder* supremacy, a move made by the majority of the top 500 companies in the world.[30] Over and above being driven by the financial crisis, this move recognises that business cannot be sustainable if it serves only the interests of shareholders. On another level, South Africa has been on this course since before the democratic elections due to the recognition of the crisis caused by apartheid.

The new approach suggests an expression of the inter-dependence of the actor groups, given the recognition that business cannot be sustainable if it only focuses on profit-making. A mix of the crisis in education, the national challenge of inequality and the private sector's concern about the continuity of its profitability in the long-term motivated the actors to establish the NECT, that is, to work together based on altruistic incentives.

The crisis-related motivations for establishing the NECT have extensive threads running through several other multiple stakeholder initiatives discussed in Chapter 1. The *Freedom Charter* and the UDF were a response to the apartheid crisis; the NECC was established to restrain the fomenting crisis of students opting to put aside education in order to secure freedom; the Joint Education Trust and the NBI were set up to address the poor quality of educational outcomes of the pre-the democratic era; SANAC was established to coordinate the national response to the HIV/Aids crisis; and ASGISA to address slow economic growth and skewed beneficiation across population groups.

Improved stakeholder engagement

The NDP underscores the need for collaboration by citing that 'business, labour and civil society are diverse groupings and rarely speak with a common voice',[31] and advises that social dialogue is promoted to '[avert] dysfunctional relationships among the public and private sectors, and civil society'.[32] The South African Constitution also promotes stakeholder engagement by making a provision that 'the public must be encouraged to participate in policy-making'.[33]

Dialogue is a form of collaboration that is widely welcomed among actor groups. Commenting on the public dialogue organised by the NECT and the South African Competition Commission on school uniform price collusion, the Minister of Education cited the approach as one that would put some niggling policy matters to rest by getting people to hear each other's views and giving them an opportunity to vent. Dialogue is also recommended by

SADTU as a means to resolve government–union relationship issues, which they consider to be 'conflictual by its nature'. As cited by the SADTU interviewee, dialogue was used to amicably break the deadlock surrounding 'the annual national assessment which has been a sore point, and both sides decided ... to sit down and then come up with a task team to resolve it'.

In the same way that dialogues do, bringing people around the same table helps to build interpersonal relationships that are critical for policy engagement and implementation, and to unleash energy and skills which may be lying wasted in communities. An example is the case of the District Steering Committees that were established by the NECT and that were able to bring together over 500 professionals and representatives of society, including doctors and lawyers. The committees helped to build social capital that in turn unleashed additional skills and energy into the education improvement space. From the private sector perspective, there is a view that this sort of stakeholder engagement creates and maintains checks and balances that serve as a basis for holding the state accountable, and coordinates voices, whether from civil society organisations, organised unions or organised business.

Overall, the state uses policy to promote public participation and participation of actor groups that expect engagement with the state to address crises and development challenges. The state, teacher unions and the private sector perspectives gravitate towards a national practice of engagement to achieve various imperatives such as accessing and influencing policy-making processes, relationship-building, resource mobilisation and public accountability. These actor engagements are intended to build social capital – human development derived from social interaction that mobilises tangible and intangible assets in pursuance of a common vision.

Promotion of coordination and collaboration

Collaboration among actors in the education sector and the strengthening of the coordination of education improvement initiatives and activities were additional grounds that led the founding organisations to establish the NECT, as expressed during the leadership dialogue that preceded the NECT's founding.[34] The leadership dialogue concluded that an Education Collaboration Framework should be developed to improve the coordination of partner efforts aimed at improving education.

Improving coordination has two imperatives: better co-ordination of education support initiatives and pooling of resources. Concerning improvement of the coordination of education support initiatives, the NAPTOSA representative maintained that NAPTOSA found it necessary to join the NECT because they could not see evidence of impact from initiatives that preceded the NECT, wherein multiple organisations had 'operated in the same space and there was no coordination', and, where there was some coordination, there were signs of favouritism. In support of the coordination imperative, Minister Motshekga indicated that

> As government, we would want a place that centralises good practice. It's good for them [the private sector] to put in their money, they know the experience [or project learnings] can be used to inform and feed into government.

Collaboration is thus seen to improve the impact of education improvement initiatives, reduce favouritism and increase the sharing of good practices among actor groups involved in the education space. This observation is consistent with Graeff's assertion that 'working in groups helps to overcome particularistic tendencies created to exclude other people',[35] and that may involve competitive practices within and between actor groups.

Improved coordination also addresses the state's concern about the existence of many small projects which all demand government involvement and endorsement. These projects often work in an uncoordinated manner in support of the same schools or schools in the same circuits and districts. The need for improved coordination is expressed in the interview inputs of the state and teacher union representatives.

The call for collaboration also demonstrates the inefficiency with which the private sector organises their support in the education sector. This weak level of coordination may be associated with the competitive, self-interested nature of private sector operations. In the end, such uncoordinated efforts have negative effects on the individual schools or groups of schools targeted by the interventions. The negative effects may manifest in the form of disruptions of the intra- and inter-school timetables and programmes, and confusion regarding school cultures, content taught and methodologies used, resulting from conceptual and logistical misalignment among the multiple projects. Arguably, leaving the private sector alone to support schools advances the detested phenomenon of philanthro-capitalism,[36] which uncritically promotes business methods and approaches in the development space.

The practice of pooling resources has been another motivation for actor groups joining the NECT network. This view was expressed by the civil society representative who indicated that when the NECT was initiated, the NGO sector felt that a solution to the NGO (resourcing) crisis was emerging. He expressed the view that the establishment of the NECT presented 'hope that something that can pull all the resources together and so that [we] move with a shared vision and move together'. One can sense a self-serving sentiment in this view, wherein the envisaged pooling of resources would benefit the NGO sector. An additional perspective offered is that of a common mission among stakeholder groups and them 'moving together'.

The idea of resource pooling was expressed differently by Mugwena Maluleke, SADTU's secretary-general for 14 years. Maluleke pointed out his expectation for the mobilisation of different forms of capital to improve the quality of education. He expected business and government to bring financial resources, communities to bring the 'mobilising force', unions to bring their goodwill to 'narrow the distance from or normalise the relationship with the government and minimise disruptions', and business to mobilise other businesses to realise that having an educated citizenry is in their best interest to build a strong and stable democracy. A similar understanding is expressed by Volmink and Van der Elst, who maintain that NGOs contribute a unique form of social capital: 'NGOs are close to communities, can tap into social capital, and are able to mobilise community members in support of national imperatives'.[37]

The viewpoints expressed above by the various actor groups point to the importance of the mix of various complementary forms of capital in education development initiatives: financial, social and cultural. This conclusion is in line with the observation by the network theorists Stephen Borgatti and Daniel S. Halgrin that 'flows' in networks are the transmission of both tangible and intangible events, and are inferred forms of relational data rather than measured forms of interactions.[38] The flows go beyond resources to include beliefs and information, and their outcomes involve non-kinship relationships.

Actors' self-interest in joining the NECT network

All actors appear to enter networks with selfish motives that are tactically used to achieve their actor- or actor group-specific operational and strategic goals. In the case of the NECT, the state's self-serving interests revolved around rebuilding the credibility of the Department of Basic Education (DBE) and public education, and mediation between the DBE and stakeholders with which it had a conflictual or potentially conflictual relationship. Passionately expressing these reasons, Minister Motshekga said

> That was the big motivation about the NECT, to get South Africans of stature, and that's what also attracted me ... who are respected in the country to give endorsement to public education, just like they do in business. They get sports people to endorse the product. NECT, in that sense, [entails] the endorsement of people who have credibility.

An additional, related motivation of the state to engage in the NECT network was to use independent and senior people who were part of the NECT as referees. The referees were envisaged to umpire engagements between the DBE and organisations with which it had conflictual relationships. The DBE representative acknowledged that the DBE was 'under attack' and 'at war' with some education stakeholders, and conceded that it helped to have 'an independent voice of people' like the former Deputy-President of South Africa, 'Phumzile [Mlambo-Ngcuka, who] was a good voice because she had a high-profile office and a respected voice'. The resolution of unproductive conflict and improving the DBE's rapport with education stakeholders was one of the main grounds on which the DBE was convinced to engage in the process of establishing the NECT. As in my recollection below, reducing conflict among stakeholders was the basis on which the talks about the NECT were initiated.

> When I made a personal visit to the Minister's home in July 2012, wherein the founding conversations about the NECT ensued, part of my intentions was to address the unproductive conflicts in education. I indicated my concerns about, among other things, the high number of days the DBE spent in court defending itself against civil rights NGOs. The extended periods in court and the DBE's efforts redirected to these cases were having negative effects on the delivery of programmes. I recollect how a number of initiatives, including the national systemic evaluation, were delayed, presumably because of the distractions from the tensions between the DBE and the civil rights organisations. I suggested that we organise a dialogue at which the Minister would tell them what she could do and could not do as a national Minister and propose to the NGOs how they could assist her. This dialogue became the NECT founding leadership dialogue idea that Minister Motshekga, Sizwe Nxasana and I embraced and shaped.

The state's approach and actions in securing endorsements and mediation departed from the Weberian notion of the state as a superstructure that uses its power to dominate other stakeholders and direct the elements of economic development. The South African state demonstrates how it complements its power from outside the confines of the 'classical state' through the use of 'credentialisation' from societal networks. The emerging view supports Hagmann and Péclard's position that the state is not clearly distinguishable from civil society, and that its power is centralised in multiple power points where a wide range of actors (state and non-state) are involved.[39] In this case, the state uses other power bases to bolster its classical source of power concentrated in the institutions it controls.

Arguably, the private sector's self-interests associated with joining a network revolve around 'business sustainability'. In this regard, I posit that business sustainability is primarily sought via three strategies: (1) adhering to enforceable laws (such as licenses to operate and tax laws); (2) pursuing paid-for business contracts, which is the primary way business engages with the state; and (3) utilisation of after-tax social investment (philanthropism). Adherence to the laws ensures business compliance and therefore the legality of businesses to operate, and philanthropism presents private businesses as corporate citizens, interested in assisting the government and the people of the country. Notably, philanthropism comes with further benefits linked to tax reductions. As Gainer states, private businesses enjoy 'marketing mileage' or 'brand equity' when they engage in philanthropism.[40]

From the discussions above, it can be argued that the state and the teacher unions attach a premium to good relationships and political power; business is interested in operational sustainability and profit; and the NGOs, with no resource bases of their own, in their survival. The private sector and unions also appear to be interested in power to influence the state.

24

Biographical motivations

The personalities, histories and experiences of the founders of the NECT played a key role in the motivation for its establishment. Two of the three pre-establishment committee members had been involved in other MSOs prior to the founding of the NECT.

For instance, Minister Motshekga referred to her involvement in the NECC that, in turn, followed her activist role in society. In her reminiscence about the NECC she explained: 'I was a teacher and an activist and ... fortunately, my heart was close to it, I was teaching in Soweto. We had to organise lectures and we used to give classes at Funda college.' Funda Community College was founded on the basis of multiple stakeholder sponsors providing arts education in the aftermath of the student uprisings of 1976.

The comment by the Minister presents her personal commitment to the course of improving education. This course involves some activism, at the centre of which is community involvement, and involves multiple stakeholders. It is also worth noting that Minister Motshekga played a role in setting up the Gauteng Education Development Trust, which brought various private sector stakeholders together to support the improvement of education in the Gauteng Province.

The second example of the biographical factor playing a role in the establishment of the NECT was shared by the Business Leadership South Africa (BLSA) representative and Chairman of the NECT, Sizwe Nxasana. He cited his commitment to 'ploughing back' and his passion for education as the motivation for his involvement in the NECT as follows:

> So, I think, at a personal level, at a very deep personal level, there is a recognition that more is expected of us who benefitted from the system, post-apartheid. To do more and do our bit in building our country. So that's my point of departure at a very personal level. Because, especially given our initial policies in the democratic

> order which tended to benefit a few, and I am one of those. I just feel this real need for me to do more for the country that I have been such a beneficiary from.

Nxasana's comments point to his recognition and sense of a moral obligation to contribute in return for his having benefited from the national system. But he further linked his motivation to be part of the NECT to his passion for education; he had been a lecturer and headed several education development trusts linked to organisations where he was a business executive.

Also, the compatibility of personalities plays a critical role in the establishment of MSNs. In the same way, incompatible personalities can hinder the establishment of such networks. A NAPTOSA representative pointed out that the bad relationship that NAPTOSA had with a previous education minister was an example of how personalities inhibited collaborative efforts. He explained that the poor relations between the union and the said minister would have thwarted the chances of agreement being reached to form an organisation like the NECT.

Personal social capital is another biographical characteristic that underpins the MSA. As noted by Edward Glaeser, the creation of social capital begins at the individual level, where an individual's social capital is 'the set of social attributes possessed by an individual – including charisma, contacts and linguistic skill'.[41] Social capital attributes also correlate to years of schooling. The use of terms such as 'astute politician' and 'matured president' by union members referring to one of the teacher union leaders further points to the importance of personalities in the establishment and operationalisation of MSOs. As observed by Stinchcombe, 'the probability of [a person] or a group of [persons who] will be motivated to start an organisation is dependent on the social structure and the position of men [and women] within it'.[42] Key to the biography of the NECT's founders was their social and cultural capital. All the founding members had senior positions in society and had been involved in similar community initiatives.

Conjuncture of policy and planning

Several of the actors suggested that they had been encouraged to engage with the NECT because of a series of developments at the time that made the context conducive to establishing the NECT. The adoption of the NDP in August 2012 created an environment in which fresh attempts could be made at improving the lives of South Africans. The overarching aim of the NDP was 'to eliminate poverty and reduce inequality by 2030' through efforts that entailed 'drawing on the energies of its people, growing an inclusive economy, building capabilities, enhancing the capacity of the state, and promoting leadership and partnerships throughout society'.[43]

The NDP created a suitable environment for the establishment of multiple stakeholder initiatives by defining the need and the vision for change and making a clarion call for partnerships. Furthermore, the NDP was adopted in a national legislative environment that promoted partnerships, as Sizwe Nxasana pointed out

> Companies were required by law to introduce [Corporate Social Investment] … between 1994 and say 2000 … Between 2000 and 2005, new BEE legislations were introduced … That's why we saw a lot of endowments that sit in broad-based empowerment schemes. There is probably R55 billion sitting in the country where probably 80% of it goes to education.

Another element of the conducive environment was the legislation which incentivised the private sector to establish social improvement programmes and measures, for example tax laws that allowed for tax rebates, the awarding of preferential bidding points for government work through complying with Broad-Based Black Economic Empowerment (BBBEE) legislation, and operational legislation such as mandatory skills development spending. Incentivising the establishment of funding sources for social development and creating a conducive legal environment was critical for the establishment of the NECT.

Added to the positive environmental factors were negative ones. The hostile environment associated with the crisis situation discussed earlier created urgency for setting up the NECT. Thus, the mix of positive and negative contextual factors contributed to the establishment of the NECT. My personal account below demonstrates this 'alignment of the stars':

> I and the Education Advisory Committee at JET Education Services were concerned about the state of education delivery, in particular, the delay and cancellation of government contracts and the large amount of time that the DBE spent in court defending itself against civil rights NGOs. During my discussion of the challenge with the Minister of Education, she told me of a similar approach from the then CEO of FirstRand who she was meeting in a few days to discuss possible support of the sector from FirstRand. Interestingly, I had received a call from the CEO of FirstRand the week before. He wanted me to assist him with setting up his family trust's education programme. From then, the three of us met no less than twice a month for close to a year to manage the setting up of the NECT.

The 'alignment of the stars' entailed a sequence of events and a timely combination of the crises in education, the release of additional resources for development through BBBEE, the adoption of the NDP which proposed fresh actions and promoted partnerships, and the meeting of people passionate about education improvement.

Building trust-based relationships

Building relationships and trust is the golden thread that ran through most actor groups' motivations to participate in the

NECT. Minister Motshekga cited 'trust deficit' as something that government always suffers from. She consequently suggested the one 'wants somebody to be a referee between you and a society in those trust deficit situations'.

Similarly, the other actor groups acknowledged high levels of suspicion of each other and a lack of trust as the dominant perceptions they had prior to engaging in the NECT network. Commenting from a business perspective, Sizwe Nxasana reminisced that companies' involvement in CSI 'started off with significant trust deficit' and that companies engaged only because they were required to by law.

Similar concerns about poor relationships between the teacher unions and government, and between government and civil rights NGOs were raised by the other actor groups. Minister Motshekga described the relationships in 2013 prior to the establishment of the NECT as 'rocky' and likened the period to being 'at war'. As mentioned, Basil Manuel, the director of NAPTOSA, referred to the relationship between unions and government prior to the setup of the NECT as a 'cat and dog' relationship. Moreover, SADTU maintained in its vision that

> The reality of SADTU being birthed as part of the struggle against apartheid and its creation "Bantu education" as well as the legitimate need to unionise teachers, posits SADTU in an inherently adversarial relationship with government [which] needs to be redefined.

Fear of being left outside the power network

The establishment of both the NECC and the NECT provide instructive evidence that actors join MSOs because of the fear of being isolated – colloquially expressed by millennials as FOMO or 'fear of missing out'. FOMO did not start with millennials. Minister Motshekga recounted that when the NECC was set up with the task of coordinating education activities in a crisis situation, it had to choose who to work with across the political continuum. In this regard, the ANC advised that the NECC should not isolate itself from the powerful players. She reported that the ANC leadership in Zimbabwe called the NECC organisers and said:

> [A]s the National Union of South African Students you are on the extreme left … you can't be such purists. It doesn't work that way. These people that you are isolating have got more people than yourselves … they said how many members do you have, you can't change the system if you have [a small number of people], you must go to the big organisations that have more members; don't isolate yourselves.

The fear of being left out of the power network was satirically expressed by NAPTOSA representative Basil Manuel. Asked why his teacher union decided to join the network, he responded

> The selfish motive. You can't be on the outside. If you are an outsider, you're just throwing stones … [and] if you throw stones at every dog that barks, you will never reach your destination.

The actor group's interest in the power to influence decisions is evident in the two examples discussed above. The sources of power in the two examples are membership numbers and positioning inside the network perceived to wield power. The behaviour of teacher unions can also be understood as the fear of what Putman called 'bowling alone', which describes the decline of social capital in the United States. Individual actors and actor groups of the NECT wanted to avoid 'bowling alone'.[44]

It can be argued from the discussion above that actors' motivations to get involved in MSA networks are driven by their interest in power and the increased impact of their education improvement activities. First, averting being left out of powerful networks enables actors to influence and exercise power from within the networks. Second, pooling resources enables the actors to access each other's power bases. On the other hand, better coordination of projects and development initiatives increases the efficiencies and economies of scale that, in turn, enable all actors to achieve their unique existential imperatives.

It can also be discerned that while trust comes across as the ultimate intended outcome of actor engagements, it is also a condition for actors to engage. As discussed above, the social capital of the individual founders of the NECT and their respective institutional linkages created the 'trust base' on which to convince the various organisations to support the establishment of and participate in the NECT network. Again, the trust base was created from outside the state, which is contrary to the NDP's view that '[t]he private sector is expected to participate in the collaborative space involving the state and other actors where cooperation is based on "trust" and "confidence" built by the state'.

Besides the different views about how trust is created, all actors involved in establishing the NECT attached a premium to good relationships and trust. Building trust-based relationships to counter trust deficit and poor relationships were the reasons the actors established the NECT.

Conclusions from the research

To sum up the research findings, a common history among the actors appears to have been central to creating organisational ideations amenable to co-establishing or joining the NECT. The ideations of NECT's founding organisations, which include being the archetypes of what they stand for, their *raisons d'être*, identities and levels of agency, determined the organisations' amenability to being party to the start of or joining the NECT.

Important conclusions that can be drawn from the discussion above are: (1) the ideations of the actor groups in the NECT network were perceived differently within and across the actor groups; (2) most actor group ideations were informed by a common history and practices (heritage) and common social values (such as the promotion of social justice) which incentivised actors to collaborate in an altruistic way; and (3) the actor groups thus took on new, non-classic roles such as the private sector actor group championing the transformation agenda and the state actor group accommodating other actor groups in undertaking its mandates.

Furthermore, the actors' and actor groups' motivations to participate can be organised into three categories: (1) contextual motivations (e.g. crises in education, conducive policy environments and existence of social capital); (2) interest in promoting stakeholder engagement aimed at building social trust and coordination of improvement efforts; and (3) self-interest such as the potential for increased power, involvement and influence in public policy and programmes.

The motivations for establishing the NECT described above are consistent with the Tocquevillian view that the capacity of society to produce social capital is determined by its 'long term experience of social organisations, anchored in historical and cultural experiences'.[45] As argued in the preceding sections, using the MSA as an approach to development is unequivocally promoted by the South African Constitution and policies that encourage public participation, engagement and collaboration. The long-standing culture of multiple stakeholder initiatives that was cultivated around the resistance to apartheid accounted, to a large degree, for the affinity of the actor groups for the MSA. In this way, the social structure based on South Africa's unique history created a conducive environment for the formation of social capital. Trust based on the credibility and social capital of individual founding members was used to bridge the trust deficit among the actor groups and to develop a generalised trust that has kept the NECT network going.

Finally, it is also observed that even where actor groups shared heritage and common social goals, they still pursued their unique self-interests, for instance, increasing their legitimacy and power in the education network.

The complex interplay of the factors discussed above inform the characterisation and behaviours of actor groups in MSNs. The next chapter dwells on the meaning, characteristics and behaviours of MSA collaborations.

Observables

The MSA involves non-commercial and multiple engagements with stakeholders. Engagement is based on reciprocal obligations, mutual accountability, sharing of investments and reputational risk, and on actor group commitments to taking joint responsibility in the design and execution of activities to create 'public good value'. Collaborations are born out of favourable social conditions. Social structures and societal dynamics such as pre-existing ties, social capital and heritage determine the grounds for the formation of MSNs and provide the values on which basis actor groups engage.

Starting an organisation involves the disruption of existing social arrangements, a result of healthy social convulsions. The founding of the NECT brought out new types of motivations for people and organisations to work together, and Box 2 provides some of the lessons learnt for promoting collaborations.

Box 2: Lessons for forging collaborations

- New collaborations are results of social convulsions, which are healthy in a normal society and are worth taking advantage of.

- Crises signify a need for new solutions in society. As such, crises should not be seen as ends in themselves, and neither should they be ignored. Even conditions of trust-deficit are opportunities for building trust and social capital. Crises are nothing but a series of tipping points of multiple tensions in society.

- The culture of dialogues and commitment to public policy participation are critical for initiating and maintaining collaborations.

Box 2 ctd.

- Collaborations provide a platform for the scaling up and improved efficiencies and effectiveness of development initiatives. They enable pooling of material and non-material resources critical to driving social change and promoting alignment of views and intentions among actor groups.

- Actor groups start and maintain collaborations if they feel that the networking meets their own needs, i.e. over and above the communal benefits. Therefore, collaborations are markets where resources are traded for self-interest and public good.

- Personal social capital is the source from which societal social capital germinates. The start of new collaborations is dependent on the positions that the initiators hold in society as figureheads. Stinchcombe proposed as early as 1965 that social structure and the position of men [and women] within it will motivate them to start organisations.

3.

Collaboration
Dynamic Manifestation of
Mutual Values, Power and Positioning

Multiple stakeholder networks (MSNs) and approaches (MSAs) are like organisms with unique characteristics, emotions and behaviour drivers. In this chapter, I explore the characterisation of the MSA in terms of the social conditions for the formation of MSNs and the structural (or network) and social forms that the network took in the case of NECT. I then shed some light on the actor group behaviours.

Characterisation of the NECT as an MSA collaboration

The MSA and public–private partnerships

Partnerships generally entail a new role where the government is no longer the regulator and sole provider of solutions but becomes a participant in a self-regulating network.[46] Partnerships bring institutional change that entails a move from 'government' to 'governance', characterised by a polycentric state with multiple centres, more decentralisation than central administration, inter-agency working rather than departmentalisation, and innovation rather than the rule-following characteristic of bodies established in the corporatist period.[47] Partnerships in development should be conceived to cover numerous categories:

government to government, public–private partnerships, and multiple stakeholder partnerships. Government-to-government partnerships are designed around official development assistance (ODA), an approach that seeks to improve donor harmonisation, alignment with the recipient's policies and enhanced aid effectiveness, predictability and accountability.[48]

Another category of partnerships distinguishable from the MSA is the public–private partnership (PPP). PPPs symbolise a retreat from privatisation and a move to a mixed economies approach to development. As argued by Ginsburg, MSNs are distinguishable from PPPs by their non-contractual nature, that is, they do not involve service level contracts with the specification of the quantities and quality of outputs and outcomes for which payments will be made in a specific period.[49] The MSA differs also on the basis that it does not entail definable commercial benefit for the private provider.

The MSA involves actors from the private sector and the public sector in a process that entails reciprocal obligations and mutual accountability, sharing of investments (financial or in-kind) and reputation risks, and joint responsibility for the design and execution of activities. It differs from the kinds of contractual partnerships that involve services such as infrastructure delivery partnerships, private operations of public schools, outsourcing of services, innovation and research partnerships, and voucher and subsidy systems.[50]

A review by Tony Butcher of the Education Action Zones partnerships in the United Kingdom[51] suggests that the analysis of partnerships alters the bias of the term partnership from the synchronic to a temporal perspective. In other words, the understanding of the MSA should focus on how partnerships form, reform and sustain themselves. Butcher suggests that partnership is 'a process of contested change or, more tentatively, as a stage in the demise of one form of organisation and in the possible emergence of another'.[52]

Main features of MSA collaborations

The MSA is primarily not government-led; it does not entail commercial beneficiation for the private sector players; it entails rather a rethink of government engagement with other actor groups and can be under-stood as a contested process where some players replace others in the development space.

The MSA as a form of social capital

The discussion in the preceding chapter highlighted that the adoption of the MSA is dependent on the existence of trust and social capital, where national history is a factor of both.

Social capital entails the connectedness of people or organisations that is based on a common mission and common values, norms and sanctions which are used to create social value. Just like human cultural and physical capital, social capital makes it easier to achieve certain ends or future benefits for some individuals. Social capital theorists hold the view that the production of social capital entails an interplay of network actors affected by inequalities of power and resources and by conflict over the influence of the network.

In the NECT case study, there is extensive evidence of social capital playing a role in the establishment and operationalisation of the NECT. There is also evidence confirming the existence of the building blocks of social capital that are posited in the literature: social norms; reciprocity; trust and sanctions. The promotion of social justice appears to have been the primary social norm that incentivised the actors to join the NECT.

The evidence from the NECT on the role of trust playing an intermediary role and serving as a central feature of social capital is mixed. Instead, the NECT was established in the context of an inter-actor trust deficit, that is, weak political trust. The representatives of the state, the teacher unions and private sector (and funding partners in particular) expressed the lack of trust among themselves as the reason they considered collaborating. There is, however, evidence that the individual trust and personal social capital of the founding members formed the basis for the establishment of the NECT. In this case, the biographical profiles of the founding members, characterised by their personalities, histories and networks, were used to create the trust required to establish the NECT.

There is also limited evidence of the role of sanctions as a tenet of social capital in the NECT network. Evidence can be observed as far as it relates to the credentialisation of the actor groups in the network. Using Halpern's argument that sanctions can be weak or strong, positive or negative, credentialisation can be categorised as a weak but positive incentive since it is not implemented officially nor is it directly usable by the actor groups to access other benefits.[53] In the NECT case, none of the actor groups or the secretariat could sanction any of the other actor groups. However, some wanted the credentials of being associated with the NECT.

National heritage as a necessary condition for the establishment of an MSA collaboration

The role of national heritage in the establishment of an MSA collaboration was hypothesised in Chapter 1, where national heritage was highlighted as being the reason behind the establishment of several political, educational and social development multiple stakeholder initiatives such as the UDF, NECC and SANAC. Heritage is a strong societal variable that is based on a unique ensemble of societal experiences including shared history, institutions, practices, personalities, folk memories, and literary associations among communities, groups and individuals. It is recognised and enjoyed by specific consumers, who may be actual or latent.[54] While the historic practices of the MSA in South Africa arguably promoted the establishment of the NECT, the state, on the other hand, played a critical role in promoting the NECT and other forms of collaboration through its policies and pronouncements such as the NDP.

The MSA as a network

Networks are a structural manifestation of the MSA. According to network theorists, a network comprises actors, each with their own agency but also connected via various kinds of ties to form a definable structure.

The actor groups that make up the NECT had distinct agency roles in society but came together to establish strong ties based on a common commitment to improving the quality of education. However, the widely held understanding in the NECT that the organisation consists of the four actor groups – state, labour, business and civil society – is challenged by network theorists. For example, Latour holds the view that networks have a boundaryless, 'fibrous, thread-like, wiry, stringy, ropey, capillary character that can never be captured by the more structured approaches'.[55] Latour's view demonstrates the complexity and nebulousness of the membership in a MSA collaboration. The principle of boundarylessness means that even the education actors and actor groups that are not signed up to the NECT are technically part of the NECT network. Within this understanding, networks should not be treated as a group with absolute boundaries. An unconnected node should be seen simply as a weak tie due to its distant positioning. Such a node holds the potential for strengthening the network's connection to other networks. This postulation suggests that NECT membership recruitment should not be limited to those who already share common values with the founders and the existing members of the network.

However, the boundaryless concept contradicts the views of representatives of state and civil society regarding the representation of smaller teacher unions. They expressed the view that smaller teacher unions did not matter much and that the representation of actor groups with smaller constituencies should be kept to a minimum. They favoured embracing organisations that represent bigger constituencies and argued that such organisations had direct relevance to the work of the

NECT since they represented more voices. While it is important to keep the network membership limited to ensure effective coordination, an instructive principle emerging from the NECT case study is that participation in the network should not be only on the strength of shared traits – social homogeneity or power of actors – since networks are arguably stronger and more sustainable if they do not connect only those with already strong ties.

Both the literature and the analysis of empirical data from the NECT suggest that actors in networks tend to have pre-existing ties before they are joined formally through organisations. As observed by Pachauri, 'partners are networked because ... of their individual histories of collaborations and alliances amongst themselves.'[56] Therefore, a formal establishment of a network organisation entails strengthening pre-existing ties. In this way, pre-existing levels of non-political trust are extended; and the pattern of the flows of resources is changed. This was found to be true in the case of the NECT, where all the founders were connected to or had pre-existing ties with other organisations. Founding members and patrons of the NECT had been involved in the NECC, were senior members of the ruling party or had been part of an earlier education improvement process.

Another perspective on the structure of networks emanating from the case study of the NECT is that the MSA involves a set of nested networks. Below is a simplified representation of the NECT actor networks, comprising just the four actor groups under discussion. The figures both represent transactions between these four groups. Figure 1a outlines the NECT as a web of the actor groups at a macro-level and shows the artificial boundary encompassing the officially signed-up actor groups. In this figure, ties between the nodes are the official traceable flows such as financial, technical and political relationships.

Figure 1b, on the other hand, demonstrates how actor groups themselves are made up of a network of actors – therefore creating networks within networks. For instance, the private sector actor group is made up of different business associations

(BLSA, Business Unity South Africa, etc.) which are, in turn, made up of various business organisations. The same applies to the union actor group, which is made up of teacher union blocks and different union organisations with unique ideations. The state, in turn, is made up of various departments at national and provincial levels. The civil society actor group is no different. The NGOs, for instance, belong to various sub-groupings and associations which are organised according to the nature of the programmes they run (e.g., civil rights organisations, organisations dedicated to teacher training or specific subject areas or that specialise in particular education phases such as early childhood education). The large actor groups such as the DBE and teacher unions also have multiple tiers nested within them in the form of national, provincial and regional tiers, each of which has a different delegated level of authority. The various tiers of the multi-tier bureaucracies bring different dynamics into the nested networks of actor groups.

MSA networks are further complicated by the multiplicity of interactions and flows among the actors and their actor group,

Figures 1a & b: Depiction of the NECT macro and micro-level networks

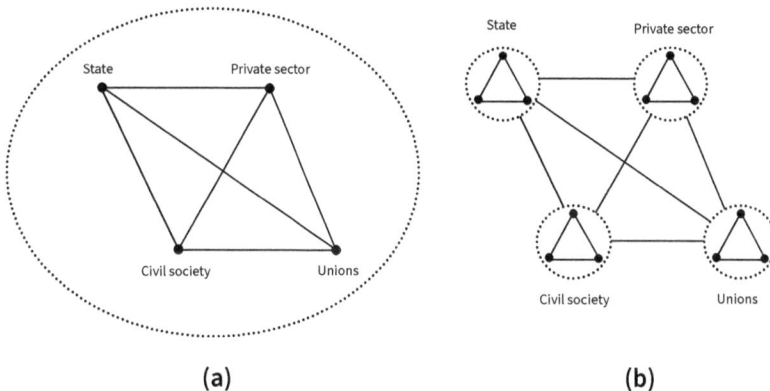

(a)   (b)

which tend to form a mesh of multi-directional connections between actors. Figure 2 depicts the further complex interactions and flows that can manifest among actors. In such a mesh of transactions, secondary nodes emerge among the defined NECT actors and the actor groups. A secondary node can be a consultative forum between the DBE and the teacher unions, other related stakeholders such as the school governance structures or conferences that create unique ties. Secondary nodes are not aligned to network boundaries or officially connected nodes. Secondary nodes would not follow the NECT actor group network configuration. They may be observable or abstract and their flows may be the same or different from those that flow in the primary nodes. This means that the traffic may vary from that which manifests within the artificially delineated boundaries such as that of the NECT members. For example, teacher unions and the DBE may engage on educational issues in the education sector but also on political issues with political parties.

Figure 2: Depiction of multi-directional and tiered networks

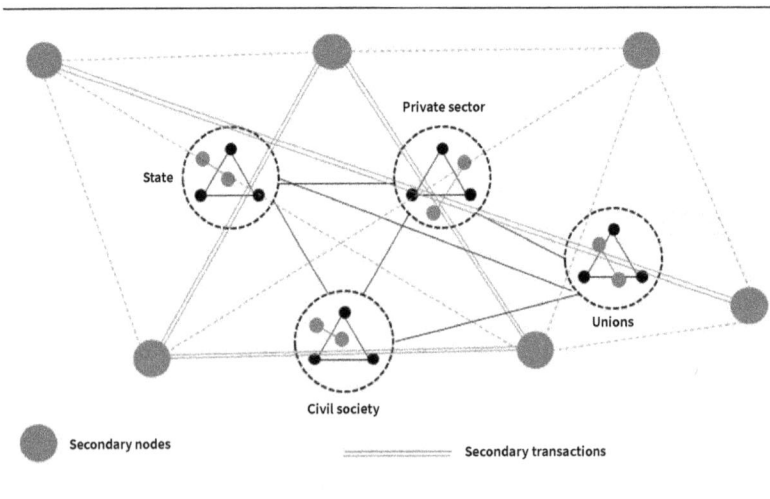

In reality, there is no network with a fixed delimitation because social capital has low controllability.[57] Therefore, in managing networks, focus should be on *influencing* the patterns and flows rather than on *controlling* them. This means, for example, that the NECT would be more sustainable if its secretariat moved its attention from structured, delineated interests to influencing as many nodes as possible. Influence requires the flexible, self-organised steering of multiple actors driven by mutual interdependences.[58] To influence networks, actors and the network secretariat should vie for the most 'salient positioning' in the network and thereby gain the power to influence the actors. '[O]ne can only gain leverage over a network by first changing one's position to one that is more salient … [to] exploit a structural hole or secure a central position'.[59]

Overall, the characterisation of the MSA discussed in this subsection distinguishes MSA collaboration from the other forms of PPPs.

Network characteristics of the MSA

- MSA entails non-contractual coalitions of willing people and/or organisations bound by common motivations, incentivised by interest in 'public good' value and driven by sets of common values.

- It involves the strengthening of pre-existing ties and the establishment of multi-directional, multi-tier, boundaryless networks that are more easily managed via influence rather than control measures.

The operationalisation of the MSA

To understand the relationships among the NECT actors and to explain the engagement dynamics of actor groups in the NECT network, I used insights from network theory. Network theory is built on the understanding that networks can be better understood by their relatedness and interactions and not just by the attributes of the actors themselves, which is the focus of other foms of research. I thus used inter-relational data and actors' environments to trace the relationships and power dynamics among actor groups and their resultant positioning in the NECT network. I consciously took as the starting point that relationships and networks are complex, non-hierarchical interactions that should be understood by exploring their characteristics beyond their structures. The understanding of these engagements entails social relationships comprising dynamic flows of tangible and intangible assets.

I collected and analysed actor groups' self-perceptions of their engagement factors and their perceptions of the other actor groups' engagement factors to discern how the actor groups engaged with each other. I sought, through this process, to build an understanding of (1) each actor group's perceptions of its own actor group (intra-actor group perspective); (2) the other actor groups' perceptions and experiences of each actor group (inter-actor group perspective); and (3) a synthesis that suggests a set of group-specific drivers and common drivers (across actor groups) which inform how the actor groups engage with each other.

The actor group's self-perceptions and how they are perceived contribute towards the groups' identities, agency profiles and power that they use to engage with each other. Thus, the power dynamics among the actor groups, the manifested positions they occupy in the network, and the behaviour incentives and disincentive in the network – behaviour drivers – can be used to understand how multiple stakeholder networks operate.

The perceptions of actor groups I discerned based on both the actor group self-perceptions and the perceptions of others are briefly presented below.

The state as the most powerful superstructure

Both the state actor group itself and the non-state actor group perceived the state as a powerful superstructure that is in control, whose power needs to be kept in check or accessed in order to reach other actor groups' goals. Four driving factors behind the state's engagement with the other actor groups could be identified. These revolved around the state's well-recognised power, the state's interest in maintaining its legitimacy, the state's recognition of its inherent capacity gaps, and the resultant incentive for the state to collaborate with other actor groups to close its capacity gaps in order to meet its policy development and service delivery obligations. Because of its large size, resources and constitutional authority, the state performs some exclusive functions in society that none of the other actors can, such as policy-making and enforcement. Its large size, while advantageous, is also perceived to inhibit it from optimally innovating and to contribute to its blind spots; for instance, unlike the teacher unions who are directly connected to the teachers, the state does not tap into sub-networks effectively.

Brand equity or social development-driven private sector?

Both the private sector/funders representative and the other actor groups perceived the funder actor group's participation to be driven by a combination of moral obligations linked to improving the country and the private sector's sustainability interests. The funder actor group's sense of moral obligation and the need to meet the publicly prized standard of corporate citizenship account for much of the group's motivation to carry out philanthropic activities. The non-private sector actor group expressed a sceptical view of the private sector actor group. The group's involvement in philanthropy was seen as being primarily driven by profit and power, and a desire to influence the way the development sector works, that is, as philanthrocapitalism – the tendency to promote private sector approaches and allow the private sector to vie for co-governance, wrestle with the state for power and seek marketing rewards or brand equity from corporate social engagements.

The funder actor group's interest in education revolved around the impact of their investment programmes which is under-mined by the group's limited educational programming capacity, weak intra-actor group collaboration and an environment in which a trust deficit exists. As observed by Porter and Kramer, moral obligation as the basis on which the funders participate in development is in competition with their sustainability imperatives.[60]

The multiple silhouettes of the teacher union group

The power the unions or union actor groups wield, the sources of union power (whether from representativity or political bases), the value of the union power and the fungibility of such power into other forms of value that the other actors wished to tap into (e.g., legitimacy or inclusivity of voices), determined how the actor groups perceived the union actors and how the unions engaged with the other actors.

The teacher union actor group and its union-member actors are unique organisations characterised by broad-based power that none of the other actors enjoy. The unions have mixed organisational configurations which straddles political, professional and industrial action organisational types. Cutting across these configurations is the social justice agenda which commits union actor groups to change the social, political and economic status of learners and teachers. The social justice agenda incentives would arguably make teacher unions amenable to engaging collaboratively with actor groups that support education improvement and the achievement of the national development goals. The power and positioning of the union actor group makes it an indispensable player in education improvement networks such as the NECT, meaning that the other actor groups ought to be incentivised to engage constructively with the teacher union actor group.

The cousin in the family: civil society

The civil society actor group performs an incongruous role in the education network. Civil society actors are weak network nodes but play the powerful role of holding the state accountable. They are characterised by organisational weaknesses and weak actor group coordination but are able to perform non-exclusive roles that none of the other actor groups can, promoting solidarity, self-help, goodwill and agency, and they reach where the other actor groups can't. The civil society actor group is a zone of contestation [and] a site of structural inequalities which may constrain some actors whilst enabling others. It provides a basis for state accountability, additional capacity to co-perform state tasks, and a conduit through which development funders channel resources. It is a basis of affirmation and legitimation of citizen's rights in a democracy and of how those rights are transacted

A confluence of the incongruous profile comprising its weak network positioning, distance from the state, inherent mistrust between it and the state, and a wide suite of exclusive roles would make the civil society actor group a cautious group that negotiates rather than uses power to find its way around the network. This proposition arguably excludes those NGOs whose sole *raison d'être* is to hold the state accountable.

Power and network positioning

Power and network positioning are central influences of actor group behaviours in networks. Power is the resource that the actor groups continuously contest for in the network. It is used to access, control, manipulate, transfer resources, and to direct or influence the behaviour of others or the course of events.

The exercise of power was observed to be a central feature in the NECT network, where actor groups pursued control of each other's resources and expected some returns. For instance, the teacher unions brought the large teacher membership as a resource, with an expectation for improved credibility and access to private sector and government financial resources. The private sector brought financial resources, with an expectation of increasing their brand equity and influence on policy. The state brought its constitutional power and associated financial resources, with an interest in increasing its legitimacy and fast-tracking policy implementation. Overall, the four actor groups in the NECT were interested in pooling their various forms of resources to address educational challenges.

As discussed earlier, an actor group gains power in a network if it changes its position to one that is more salient in order to exploit a structural hole or secure a central position. Figure 3 demonstrates the concepts of network positioning and power in the context of the NECT. In Figure 2 the actors' interactions and relationships were modelled to be ubiquitous and multi-directional, assuming equality among actor groups. In reality, actor groups do not engage as equals. Rather, as depicted in Figure 3, the modelling suggests that actor group relationships were based on a pecking order among the actors, informed by each actor group's power and influence.

The actor group power and positioning mapping places the state at the top of the food-chain and civil society at the bottom. This mapping is in line with the theoretical conception of the state as a sophisticated apparatus of control. In the case of the NECT, the state is presented as an actor possessing supreme power drawn from its constitutional mandate and large financial

Figure 3: Actor-group power and network positioning map

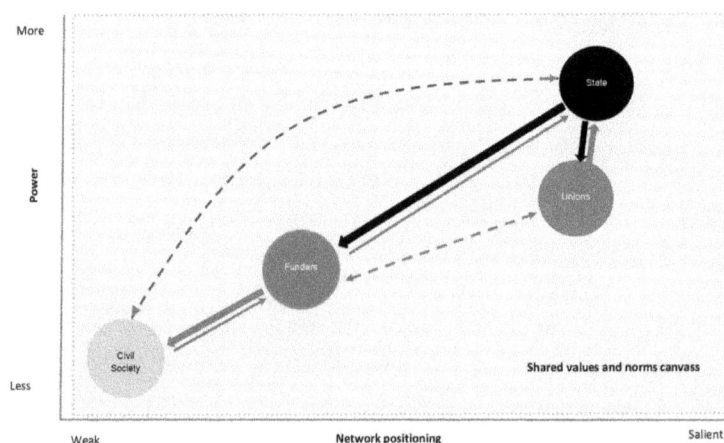

resource base. The participation of the state in the NECT network, however, presents an atypical state in the Weberian sense. Its characterisation and behaviour are closer to Hagmann and Péclard's conception of the post-colonial state which is a product of continuous negotiation between the Weberian state and the recurrent history of the African state based on African norms.[61] In an African state, power is distributed to state and non-state actors, where the state extends beyond the realm of bureaucrats, policies and institutions. In the NECT and the extended broader education network, the state serves as the point of reference for the other actor groups.

The teacher unions take the second power position in the NECT network. As discussed above, the teacher unions draw their power from their closeness to the teachers, and they are an alternative voice and force that keep the state (as the employer) in check. The salient network position of the teacher unions was recognised by all actor groups, demonstrated in the actor groups' acknowledgement of the powerful agency of the teacher unions in the education sector. The recognition of this agency was demonstrated in the NECT case study interviews by phrases such as 'teacher unions are more than stakeholders'; 'the importance of the collegiality between the Minister and the leader of the teacher unions'; and 'teacher unions are the cause of bad education outcomes'.

The teacher union actor groups' relationship with the funder actor group is indirect, weak and defined by a bidirectional sense of mistrust. The funder group was found to distance itself from the teacher unions and perceived them to be playing a pernicious role in education. This view is extensively held in society, where unions are viewed as an obstacle to education reform and a threat to the 'neo-liberalisation project'. The teacher unions, in turn, viewed the funder actor group, and the private sector in general, as a secondary player in the education space whose interest is profiteering from what should be a basic public service. The private sector interest is perceived by unions as a 'thirst for [the] huge [education] market'.[62]

Empirical data from the NECT case study presents the relationship of the funders with the state as one in which the funder actor group sought to promote its power and control of the education sector. The level of power and control the group aspired to is expressed in its definition of a development partnership, which is paraphrased to include 'leveraging public resources', 'collective voice of funders', 'strategic engagement' and 'influencing' the education vision. As observed by Gainer, the funder actor group also pursues its influence in the social development space through 'philanthrocapitalism', promoting the technical (methods and methodologies) superiority of the private sector in producing social welfare, social value and enhancing public good.[63]

The relationship between the funder actor group and the civil society actor group is an unequal one, with the civil society actor group at the receiving end. The NECT case study data presents the civil society actor group as an over-obliging one, with no dependable source of power, primarily concerned with justifying its space in the education network and playing a complementary role. The descriptions in the data project the civil society actor group as a weak node that cannot exist on its own. These observations were corroborated by the literature review in which the civil society actor group is portrayed as 'normative confusion', a gap-filler that re-emerged as a result of society's disenchantment with trade unions, and a structure that is prone to be hijacked by the middle class. Although civil society perceives itself as the sphere of solidarity, self-help and goodwill from where the state can be held accountable, both the empirical data and literature review depict civil society as a weak actor that is used by both the state and the funder actor group to achieve their goals. Civil society is used to provide additional capacity to co-perform the tasks of the state and serve as the conduit for development funding. The empirical data from the case study corroborates these observations and further points to a sense of mistrust between the state and civil society, and to the bullying of civil society by the state.

Even though the actor group relationships take the form of a pecking order, the actor groups continue to interact and influence each other in a dialectical way. All the actor groups give away some of their rights and interests in exchange for the common objectives of the network. Moreover, the groups alter their operations in order to accommodate the other players in the collaboration network. For instance, Bird observes that the state that has joined similar collaborations changes from *running a government* to *governance*.[64] According to Bird, a change to governance in the way the state engages entails an assumption of a polycentric state which departs from a centralised, departmentalised and rule-driven administration to one that is characterised by multiple centres, inter-agency working and innovation.[65] The evidence from the NECT case study confirms Bird's assertion. In the NECT's case, the state relinquished some of its authority in the education improvement space. In the shared structures, representative governance structures of the NECT such as the Board of Trustees, District Steering Committees as well as in joint programmes, the state is treated more as an equal actor, and co-governance is adopted as the organising logic.

Polycentricity is a complex form of governance, with multiple semi-autonomous centres of decision-making nested in multiple jurisdictional levels or special-purpose governance units that cut across such jurisdictions.[66] The NECT network itself created semi-autonomous centres of decision-making across the national, provincial and district levels of the education system. These centres include committees representing the members of the secretariat, independent experts and unions. The extent of authority afforded to these centres of decision-making differs by jurisdiction, depending on various dynamics such as patterns of power of the actor groups involved, absorptive capacity levels of the state and actors' interests in the projects or activities concerned.

The central feature of the centres of decision-making is the willingness of the state to devolve some of its power, responsibility and control to extra-state entities. The polycentric state, similar to the 'non-Weberian' state posited by Hagmann and Peclard, entails an arrangement where the state has retreated; where power is located in multiple points and the line between society and the state has blurred.[67]

On the whole, the attributes and relationships of the actor groups determine their ideations, power and network positions which, in turn, determine a pattern of complementary resources that are exchanged in the social network. The continuous competition for power and the dynamic exchange of (complementary) resources among actor groups continuously produce conflicts, tensions and contestations among the actor groups; and consequently, power and positioning patterns in the network are reproduced. The next section discusses how actor groups behave in these dynamic interactions.

Actor group behaviour drivers

I pointed out earlier that factors relating to the shared history of actor groups and the social capital of influential individuals most commonly motivate the establishment of multiple stakeholder organisations. Once established, additional sets of considerations inform the behaviour of the actor groups in the network. Some network theorists would maintain that network actors' behaviour is primarily informed by their interest in the resources of other actors and in response to the incentives and disincentives that are meted out by the network. Individual actors and their groups use their referent ideations to inform their behaviours in the network and how they engage with other actor groups.

A range of actor behaviour drivers could be discerned in the NECT network. They could be categorised into those that were observed by all actor groups (coded herein as 'universal behaviour drivers') and those that were observed in some actor groups and not others ('non-universal behaviour drivers'). Although the actors making up actor groups were not homogeneous, actor groups were found to respond to similar behaviour drivers. The universal behaviour drivers influenced all four actor groups, and the non-universal behaviour drivers influenced individual actor groups or sub-groups. These behaviour drivers are discussed briefly below.

Universal actor group behaviour drivers

Certain common values and development considerations inform the interactions of actor groups in a MSA network. Most of these behaviour drivers have to do with national development imperatives and are related to national heritage aspects such as history and commitment to a social justice agenda. The national development imperatives include pursuance of macro-development objectives, improvement of public governance, and the promotion of educational outcomes.

Concerning the macro-development objectives, all the actor groups in the NECT cited the NDP and the objective of growing the economy as key drivers for their engagement in the network. Regarding the improvement of governance, actor groups expressed the need to hold the state accountable, and the state representatives expressed interest in promoting participation in policy and programmes. The improvement of educational outcomes, considered to be a public good that can drive economic growth and redress, was observed to be a common driver among all four NECT actor groups.

The second category of universal behaviour drivers that has to do with national heritage entails aspects of shared history, institutions and practices among communities, groups and individuals.[68] The South African heritage of patriotism, which manifests as a movement against the detested history of segregation, was shared by all four actor groups and informed the actors' ideations and their gravitation towards collaboration. Associated with a common national heritage were the actor groups' expressions of their moral obligation to collaborate for the improvement of education, nation-building and the pursuit of the social justice agenda. BLSA saw its role as supporting the implementation of inclusive growth, a part of the efforts to redress the historic inequalities among groups. In this regard, SADTU also expressed an intention 'to reposition the African child who suffered subjugation during the apartheid era'. As per the Tocquevillian view, the capacity of society to produce social capital is determined by experiences that are 'anchored in historical and cultural experiences'.

Non-universal actor group behaviour drivers

The non-universal actor group behaviour drivers are considerations or opportunities that carry more weight for a specific actor or actor group. These drivers function for some but not all the actor groups and entail considerations or opportunities that resonate or carry more weight for a particular actor groups' ideations or *raisons d'être*. The drivers can be categorised into push factors, pull factors and comparative advantage factors.

Push factors comprise inherent circumstances that the actor groups need to change; pull factors create the potential to improve the actor's or actor group's state of affairs; and comparative advantage factors are actor's or actor group's unique operational strengths that they use as a special resource to exchange for other forms of assets in the network. The drivers are discussed below and outlined in Table 1.

Push factors

Some push factors are common to actor groups. The two common push factors found to apply to all the actor groups apart from the teacher unions were poor organisational performance of the actor group and internal organisational weaknesses relating to technical aspects of education service delivery. Poor organisational performance of the other three actor groups included underperformance in education provision in the case of the state, low returns on investment for the funder actor group and poor fundraising in the case of the civil society actor group.

In the case of internal organisational weaknesses, the state was weak in driving efficiency, innovation and making quick changes in its trajectory; the private sector actor group lacked technical sophistication and proper coordination required to achieve their investment goals; and the civil society actor group lacked the technical capacities and a strong mandate from its constituency that would put it in good stead in the education network.

Each of the actor groups had push factors that exclusively applied to that actor group. For the private sector actor group, unique push factors were the unconducive investment environment characterised by the prevalence of corruption and an ineffective public service. The single and unique push factor for the civil society actor group was the need to be perceived to be relevant and a primary actor in the education sector. This factor may be linked to the group's weak positioning in the network. Public pressure and inter-union competition for membership were the unique key push factors for the teacher union actor group.

Pull factors

Power, network salience and control were common pull factors for all actor groups. The effect of these pull factors was more pronounced in respect of the state, private sector and teacher unions. The state was attracted towards maximising power and control, which it already enjoys; the private sector sought to gain power and control in the education sector; and the teacher unions vied to defend their sector-based power and control. While all actor groups ordinarily wish for more power, the civil society actor group was preoccupied with gaining relevance, acceptance, legitimacy and better positioning in the education network.

Improved legitimacy was also a pull factor for the state. Improved brand equity was an exclusive pull factor for the private sector actor group, and positive public perception and the engendering of the professionalisation agenda were exclusive pull factors for teacher unions.

Comparative advantage factors

The differences in ideations, characteristics and profiles of the actor groups mean that specific strengths or comparative

Table 1: Individual actor group behaviour drivers

Actor groups	Push factors	Pull factors	Comparative advantage factors
State	• Failure to deliver services at acceptable levels. • Organisational weakness and incapabilities in some functions such as dialoguing and holding oneself accountable.	• Maximising power and control in the education sector. • Improvement of the legitimacy of the state.	• State's exclusive roles which no other actor can discharge, e.g. staff deployment • Stable, supreme power and network salience • Existence of leadership amenable to collaboration
Funders	• Low returns on CSI. • Weaknesses of the actor-group in technical, educational areas. • Unconducive CSI.	• Gaining power and control in the education sector. • Maximising 'brand equity'.	• Agility and flexibility of funding organisations. • Technical abilities relevant, e.g. IT
Teacher unions	• Public pressure for unions to improve education. • Competition among unions for membership.	• Improving public perception of teacher unions. • Engendering professionalisation agenda in teacher support • programmes. • Maintenance of power and network salience in the education sector.	• Broad-based power from large • teachers' membership. • Strong alternative voice to the state's. • Rapport with and control over teachers. • Widely recognised agency among (all) actor groups.
Civil society	• Perceived non-primacy of NGOs in education. • Funding/ survival pressures. • Weak mandate from actors making up the group. • Organisational weaknesses on technical elements in education improvements.	• Gaining more relevance and acceptance before the state, teacher union and actor groups. • Gaining salience in the education network.	• NGO-unique roles in society which no other actor group can discharge. • Complementarity role to the CSI • and public service delivery. • Greater level of independence from the state.

advantages were localised in each of the actor groups. The actor groups, therefore, exploited these comparative advantages to gain better network positioning, power and control in the education improvement space. The state's comparative advantages included the delineation of its exclusive roles such as the system-wide provision of schools' operational inputs, policy-making and enforcement, its stable supreme power underwritten by the Constitution and its resultant salient positioning, and the existence of leadership amenable to collaboration.

The funder actor group's comparative advantages were their agility and flexibility and technical capabilities in the education improvement space.

The teacher union actor group's comparative advantages were based on the connection with teachers which allows the group to enjoy a 'broad power base', 'rapport with teachers', an 'alternative voice' and 'agency' in the education space.

The civil society actor group's comparative advantages were in its ability to play unique and complementary roles in the education sector and be more independent than the other actor groups, although the literature warns that this group is prone to capture by the middle class and the bureaucracy and undemocratic trends.[69]

Observables

The behaviour of organisations that make up collaborations is primarily informed by their interest in accessing each other's resources, that is, over and above being driven by the same values and norms that revolve around improving the quality of the lives of South Africans.

While all four actor groups in the NECT network were driven by their commitment to contribute to South Africa's social justice agenda, each of the actor groups was motivated by unique behaviour drivers. Crudely stated, *endorsement by and better coordination of actor groups* is at the centre of government's drive to participate, *brand equity* drives the private sector engagement dynamics, *the improvement of public profile* drives unions and *operational sustainability* drives the NGOs.

The chapter outlined a range of other push, pull and comparative advantage drivers that determine the behaviour of actor groups in networks such as the NECT.

Actor group power and network positioning are the medium through which the interests and incentives of the actor groups are exercised in the network. In the NECT network, a clear-cut power food-chain could be discerned. In the food chain:

- The state, with its constitutional mandate for education delivery combined with its significantly large institutional structure and budget, is the most powerful player.
- The unions use their large membership base and semi-political engagement approach to position themselves as the second most powerful players.
- The private sector, with its unencumbered financial resources and its place in the South African economic structure, takes the third place in the food-chain.
- NGOs take the last place as they have no clear power base in education and no official mandate in the education sector. Furthermore, they have no tangible resource base to trade in the network. However, they have the ability to reach where government and the private sector cannot reach. In the end, they largely deliver the agenda of the more powerful players, the private sector and the state in particular, although their independence enables them to keep government in check. Unions tend to ignore NGOs.

4.

Managing Multiple Stakeholder Networks
Using Influence and Suasion to Manage Without Formal Authority

Much of organisational behaviour research focuses on single organisations as opposed to MSOs, also referred to as 'network organisations'. The NECT is a network organisation since it comprises several independent organisations – with their own governance structures, administration and resources. A network organisation is:

> any moderately stable pattern of ties or links between organisations or between organisations and individuals, where those ties represent some form of recognisable accountability … formal or informal, weak or strong, loose or tight, or unbounded.[70]

Jessop maintains that MSOs are distinguishable by their inherent character of heterarchy, as opposed to hierarchy, which largely applies to single, large organisations.[71] A heterarchy, in contrast, consists of 'self-organised steering of multiple agencies, institutions and systems which are operationally autonomous from one another yet structurally coupled due to their mutual interdependence'.[72] As observed by Perri et al., 'in the inter-organisational context, a manager cannot exercise authority or legitimate power to command over an organisation in which she is not employed or where she does not hold a board-level non-executive position'.[73] That is the primary challenge of managing MSOs.

In development and intergovernmental initiatives, MSOs are typically managed through secretariats. In business organisations, joint initiatives are managed by temporary multiple organisations (TMOs), 'typically set up for a specific period to deliver innovative products or services across a range of industries such as construction, infrastructure, and engineering'.[74]

Some of the principles of managing MSOs are as follows:

- The agency for managing a network will depend on four elements: power; goal formation; influencing the form of the network; and positioning strategy.
- Instead of using control as a method generally employed in a hierarchy, managing an MSO involves 'sticks, carrots, and sermons to win over actor groups – suasion rather than control'.[75]
- Those actor groups with sufficient leverage are 'most likely convert their preferences, aspirations, resentments, disappointments into the network goals'.[76]
- Network positioning strategies to secure a measure of network salience provide the greatest chance of agency or leverage over the network structure.
- Successful management requires facilitative leadership – more neutral, consensus-building approaches – and advocacy approaches which are not partisan.
- MSO management requires a continuous consciousness of the embeddedness of the secretariat (and its operations) in the parent organisations.
- MSO management involves gaining legitimacy and maintaining power and authority across the organisations making up the network.

This chapter explores the management of the MSO in an educational context. The management aspects were explored on the basis of the NECT's Learning Programmes, a large programme with direct involvement of the highest number of actor groups – funders, unions, government units (state) and NGOs (civil society). At the time of data collection, the Learning Programmes was implemented in over 16,000 schools located in 75 education districts across the nine provinces. Over 100,000 teachers and close to 1,000 of their supervisors were involved.

Two perspectives emerged from the management of the NECT MSO: contractual aspects and programme implementation aspects. The contractual elements cover the management of agreements among the actor groups, that is, legal aspects, which are reduced to written contracts between the respective actor groups and the secretariat. The implementation elements, on the other hand, cover the dynamics of designing and implementing NECT programmes, that is, the educational programme management aspects. Both aspects are critical in managing MSOs: the relationships between the actor groups are initiated and governed by contractual agreements which then create either narrow or broad operational boundaries for the implementation of the programmes.

Managing contractual relationships

The funding and legal parameters created in grant agreements determined the allowances for and the NECT secretariat's exercising of choices in the design and implementation of programmes. This is the case because the secretariat is embedded in the actor groups, especially those involved in the founding of the NECT, the parent organisations. Parent organisations resource and spell out the operational expectations for TMOs. The design dynamics following this theory are demonstrated in Figure 4.

The contractual obligations create parameters relating to the legality of the grant agreement, enforceability, risk limitation and value for money. The operational obligations entail provisions relating to how the secretariat should run its operations in relation to the technical, economic and government compliance structures of the programme. In line with Meer-Kooistra's

Figure 4: Demonstration of the legal and financial governance dynamics

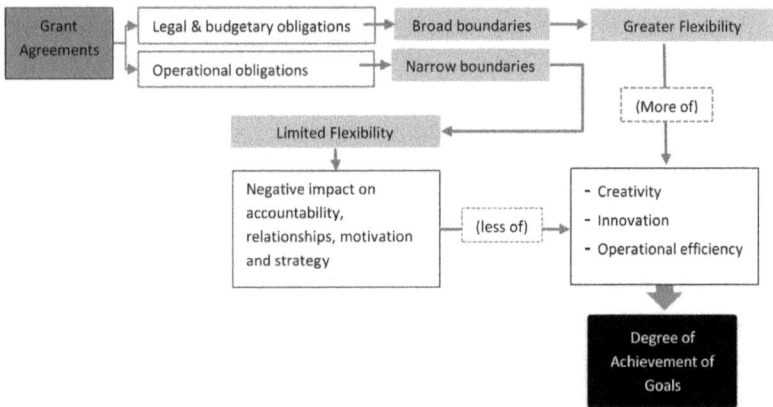

definitions,[77] the technical structure has to do with the design and implementation aspects of the education programmes, and the economic structure refers to the budgetary aspects of the programmes. The government compliance requirements, which were identified in the NECT grant agreement, refer to steps taken to ensure that the secretariat conformed to relevant laws, policies and regulations relating to training, quality assurance and qualifications.

According to the TMO body of knowledge, funding contracts that only go as far as making legal provisions create a less restrictive implementation environment or broad boundaries; and the contracts that go as far as providing bespoke or tailored operational obligations create limited operational boundaries or narrow boundaries. Broad boundaries allow for greater flexibility on the part of the secretariat which, in turn, promotes creativity, innovation and operational efficiency. Narrow boundaries, on the other hand, limit implementation flexibility and militate against the achievement of accountability, good relationships, motivation, and effective focus on strategy within the secretariat and the networks it is embedded in. Lack of flexibility is associated with the NECT's funder group's micromanagement tendencies, which include being involved in the technical and economic (or operational) structures of the TMO. This involvement blurs accountability lines between the funder group and the secretariat, undermines the professional independence of the secretariat and weakens interpersonal trust between the secretariat and the funding organisations. Furthermore, the funders' involvement in operations was found to have the potential to derail the secretariat's strategy.

The NECT case study thus confirms that the network secretariat, like the TMOs, is better managed on the basis of flexible, interpersonal processes than formal ones. This approach is corroborated by Perri et al. who hold the view that the secretariat should take the form of an 'enclave'[78] – an egalitarian organisation based on moral obligations, with weak regulation and strong integration, as opposed to a hierarchical, bureaucratic or individualistic organisation. The observation drawn from the NECT case study is that actor groups (in this case, parent organisations) that are too involved in the operations of the secretariat can cause operational inefficiencies in the secretariat and possibly restrict its impact.

Managing multiple stakeholder educational programmes

The standard project management processes of planning and controlling inputs, processes and outputs in order to achieve envisaged project benefits within scope, cost and time has further and unique requirements for network project management. Network project management involves managing a wider range of interests than single-owner project management.

Furthermore, the NECT case study revealed project management dynamics that are peculiar to education projects. The dynamics involved in educational MSOs straddle the fields of project management, education policy and theory, and stakeholder management. These sets of dynamics and issues are discussed below under two themes: (1) network programme design and (2) network project management. Programme design includes the generation of ideas to solve education problems – the technical process of formulating the initial plans for implementing the solution for the identified education problem and the ongoing adjustment of the original programme design to ensure its continued fitness for purpose. Network project management is concerned with the operationalisation of programme designs with multiple stakeholders and through multiple stakeholders' various roles.

Managing network programme design

The process of generating and adopting education solutions and programme ideation in network organisations is heavily contested. Programme design continues through the lifespan of a programme, with the designs that are adopted from such ideation processes continuously challenged and subjected to ongoing adjustments. Thus, network programme designs are in a constant state of change. Two constructs capture how the NECT managed the 'counterviews and disharmonies' involved in the continuous design processes of programme ideation management and management of programme design equilibrium.

Programme ideation management

The ideation of education solutions in network programmes is rooted in contestation among multiple actor groups. In the NECT, consultation served as the midwife that delivered and nurtured the programme designs. It was the thread that ran through the actor groups and their hierarchical levels. Consultation was used to continuously mediate power among the actor groups with interest in the programme ideation. The analysis of the NECT programme ideation processes brought to light the multi-dimensionalities of consultations and the various ends to which they were employed.

The NECT secretariat played a key role in guiding the engagement of the various players to develop a legitimate, credible programme that was approved for implementation by key and relevant players in the education system. It follows that, without the secretariat, the NECT network could not have developed programmes with sufficient support from the actor groups. I therefore conclude that having a secretariat in place and using consultations as a consensus-building tool are necessary conditions for the successful ideation of network programmes.

Maintaining the programme design in equilibrium

Similar to programme ideation and design involving contestations among actor groups and their sub-groupings, programme design is subjected to demands for continuous adjustments. First, the Learning Programme's monitoring and evaluation process advocated changes to the programme design. Second, exogenous factors such as actor groups' philosophical approaches, funders' preferences and inter-organisational competition applied continuous pressure to change the Learning Programmes design.

The various internal and external factors affecting the programme design added to the role of the secretariat. Following the choreographing of the programme ideation, the secretariat had to continue to manage the influences of the various interest groups. The continuous interplay of the different change agents meant that relevant capabilities and constant efforts were required to maintain the equilibrium of the programme design.

Given the nature of the demands and pressures for change discussed in the previous sections, I argue that the secretariat should have a mix of capabilities to enable it to deal with the change forces of a technical, ideological and theoretical nature, advanced by programme monitoring and evaluation, the demands of the teacher unions and academia and funders respectively. In such circumstances, the secretariat must be vigilant and proactive and should act in a courageous and persuasive manner that enables it to reconcile the differences among actor groups.

Network project management

Managing projects involving multiple stakeholders is different from managing projects over which an organisation has full authority and control. Managing a programme with full authority affords project managers greater leeway to plan and control inputs, processes and outputs, and to ensure that the programme delivers envisaged benefits within scope, costs and time.[79] Network programme management, which is more complex than project management where the project manager has full authority, requires sophisticated project management capabilities to manage a wide range of interests. Network programme management, which can also be seen as stakeholder management, is more about managing relationships than engaging in the classical elements of project management.

Educational project management dynamics evident in the NECT Learning Programmes can be grouped into seven conceptual categories as portrayed in Figure 5.

The seven categories of dynamics paint a picture of the aspects that need to be managed in large network programmes and provide a basis for designing the secretariat's role in such projects. Managing a network programme can be described as the art of keeping in balance multiple, often contradictory actor imperatives. It involves managing the continuous pressure to make programming changes and the endless jostling for more salient network positions among the actor groups.

A mini-model for managing education network programmes

In response to the dynamics presented in Figure 5, I propose a mini-model for MSN management. The mini-model comprises three tiers that answer three questions that emerged in the NECT case study data analysis and are deemed to illuminate how multiple stakeholder programmes are managed:

Figure 5: Demonstration of the legal and financial governance dynamics

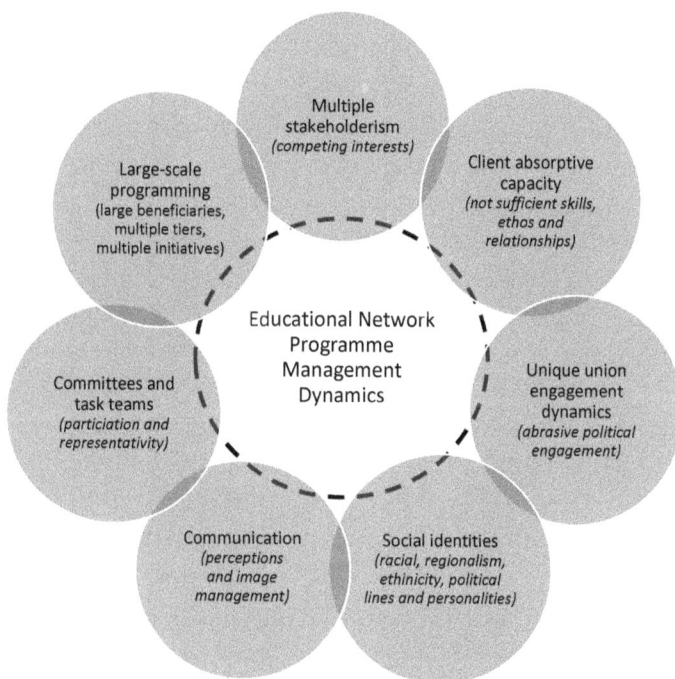

1. What is managed in educational MSN programmes?
2. Why is it important to manage the specific management considerations (referred to as fundamentals of MSN management)?
3. How does the secretariat manage MSN network dynamics?

Tier 1: What is managed in educational multiple stakeholder programmes?

The network management mini-model consolidates the MSN dynamics that relate to programme implementation into three categories of management dynamics: (1) technical programming dynamics, (2) organisational dynamics, and (3) visioning-related management dynamics. These categories are discussed below and illustrated in Figure 6.

Technical programming dynamics

Four technical programming dynamics were identified in the NECT case study: (1) the process of ideating solutions to education challenges; (2) the design of the solutions; (3) the implementation of the designs; and (4) operations management. As discussed in earlier sections, the implementation of the programme designs involved a continuous process of maintaining the programmes in states of equilibrium. MSN educational programmes are in constant states of change due to ongoing contestations among the actor groups. These contestations are characterised by continuities and discontinuities of educational philosophies and methodologies underpinning the programming, and by tensions emanating from the competing actors' paradigmatic outlooks and the various operational demands the actor groups have on the programme.

The existence of relevant technical capabilities in the secretariat is critical for managing the technical dynamics of the network. In the NECT, these capabilities were used specifically to analyse evidence about paradigms that existed at the point of designing the programme. The evidence, which included education policy, research, theory and evaluation reports, was considered as part of the programme ideation. In addition, relevant technical capabilities were utilised to create new sets of evidence through tests, pilots and evaluations in order to inform the ongoing alignment of the programmes, which emanated from the interplay of various endogenous and exogenous forces of change.

The organisational dynamics of MSN organisations

The second category of technical programme dynamics making up the model is operations management. In the case of the NECT, operations management is important given the large scale of the programme's roll-out. Managing programmes with annual

Figure 6: Multi stakeholder network management mini-model

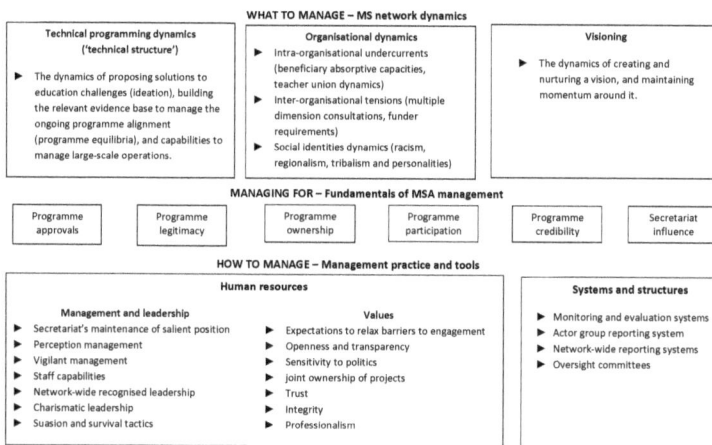

WHAT TO MANAGE – MS network dynamics

Technical programming dynamics ('technical structure')	Organisational dynamics	Visioning
▶ The dynamics of proposing solutions to education challenges (ideation), building the relevant evidence base to manage the ongoing programme alignment (programme equilibria), and capabilities to manage large-scale operations.	▶ Intra-organisational undercurrents (beneficiary absorptive capacities, teacher union dynamics) ▶ Inter-organisational tensions (multiple dimension consultations, funder requirements) ▶ Social identities dynamics (racism, regionalism, tribalism and personalities)	▶ The dynamics of creating and nurturing a vision, and maintaining momentum around it.

MANAGING FOR – Fundamentals of MSA management

Programme approvals	Programme legitimacy	Programme ownership	Programme participation	Programme credibility	Secretariat influence

HOW TO MANAGE – Management practice and tools

Human resources

Systems and structures

Management and leadership	Values	Systems and structures
▶ Secretariat's maintenance of salient position ▶ Perception management ▶ Vigilant management ▶ Staff capabilities ▶ Network-wide recognised leadership ▶ Charismatic leadership ▶ Suasion and survival tactics	▶ Expectations to relax barriers to engagement ▶ Openness and transparency ▶ Sensitivity to politics ▶ Joint ownership of projects ▶ Trust ▶ Integrity ▶ Professionalism	▶ Monitoring and evaluation systems ▶ Actor group reporting system ▶ Network-wide reporting systems ▶ Oversight committees

participation of over 20,000 teachers from nine provinces requires erudite operational and technical capabilities and systems.

Organisational dynamics, broadly, involve managing relationships and the capacity gaps that exist within and between the various actor groups. Three categories make up the organisational dynamics of MSN organisations: (1) intra-actor group organisational dynamics; (2) inter-actor group organisational dynamics; and (3) the dynamics of social identities.

The first category, *intra-organisational dynamics*, has to do with internal organisational undercurrents that manifest within actor groups. These include, for instance, contestations and competition among SADTU members during the intra-union election race. These intra-union dynamics were found to create an incentive for SADTU members to take a hard stance against the NAPTOSA programming in Bohlabela district. This was so because specific members used the programme as a basis to demonstrate their power and suitability for leadership positions.

A second example of intra-organisational dynamics at play is the dynamics among 'multi-tier actor group organisations' such as the teacher unions and the state. In the multi-tier actor groups, power and authority are negotiated between the various tiers of the actor groups, creating complex organisational dynamics. For example, the SADTU regional leadership suspended the implementation of the Learning Programmes without the knowledge of the SADTU national office. As a result, the suspension was reversed when the national leadership intervened.

The third example involves the varying levels of the Department of Education's absorptive capacity. Sub-optimum absorptive capacity was identified as an issue of concern in the Bohlabela district, where broad district leadership and their ability to withstand the influence of the unions was of concern.

Funder preferences is another example of organisational dynamics in educational MSN organisations. As discussed earlier, funders may create broad or narrow operational boundaries for the secretariat, thus adding complexity to the dynamics that the secretariat has to manage. The secretariat has to be sensitive and responsive to these internal actor dynamics in order to achieve the required programme and network outcomes.

The second category, *inter-organisational dynamics,* is characterised by the interplay of the different actor groups' ideations and the actor group behaviour drivers discussed earlier. The different ideations bring with them different engagement requirements and expectations from the various actor groups. A case in point is the observation that teacher unions are quasi-political organisations characterised by a mix of political, professional and bargaining roles. Linked to their ideation, teacher unions expect to be engaged through negotiations, are abrasive in their engagement and use political tactics to engage with other stakeholder groups.

Multi-dimensional consultations is another organisational dynamic that faced the secretariat, and entailed conducting consultations laterally between actor groups and between units within actor groups and vertically across the tiers of the actor groups – national, provincial and regional/district.

The third category, *social identity dynamics,* manifests within and across actor groups and permeates the MSN in its nested form. Social identities are a result of cultural, racial and political affiliations and determine the strengths of group relationships and trust within and between actor groups.

In the NECT case study, the social identity dynamics manifested in the forms of racism, regionalism, tribalism, political orientations and personalities. The exercise of regionalism and racism was observed between the district officials and the programme manager who was from a different racial group and province. Tribalism was displayed by some local people towards the programme management, who was blamed for hiring more people from the Xitsonga group. Political orientations played out when some teacher unions were negatively dealt with by other unions and actor groups. The social identity dynamics of parent organisations played out in the NECT network and secretariat operations and had both positive and negative impacts on the relationships, depending on the personalities of the managers involved at various points.

Visioning in MS network organisations

Visioning is the third aspect that had to be managed by the secretariat. As purported by Senge, 'few, if any, forces in human affairs, are as powerful as a shared vision'.[80] According to Senge, visioning is not a one-off exercise aimed at solving a problem but rather a continuous process of maintaining a vision built on the many visions of individual members of an organisation or, in the case of an MSN organisation, many visions of individual organisations. Thus, it is more appropriate to talk of *visioning* rather than a vision.

In the case of the NECT, evidence of visioning could be found in elements of ideating solutions to education challenges, demonstrating the potential of the ideas through pilots and tests that created evidence of success, maintaining the vision by protecting it from the many contestations, and maintaining momentum among the implementing staff, the beneficiaries and actor groups. The NECT secretariat had to build and maintain the vision. For instance, the DBE and the teacher unions were initially not interested in the Learning Programmes that would subsequently be rolled out in over 75% of the school system. In response, the secretariat undertook several processes such as joint research with the teacher unions which demonstrated the programme's worth.

Tier 2: What are the purposes of managing the specific dynamics of network programmes?

The second tier of the mini-model comprises six key management purposes referred to as 'MS Management Fundamentals'. These are approvals, legitimation, ownership, participation, credibility, and influence. Their meanings are defined below.

1. Programme *approvals* relate to the green light obtained from the actor groups regarding various design and implementation decisions.
2. Programme *legitimation* makes decisions or actions acceptable to a group of actor groups or beneficiaries. In the NECT case, approvals and legitimation were sought from the more powerful actor groups: the state and the teacher unions. Over and above the district's approval, SADTU was expected to approve the NAPTOSA programme in Bohlabela district. While the state had to approve the programme, SADTU's power drawn from its significant membership base was used to legitimate the programme.
3. Programme *ownership* relates to the sense of association that the actor groups and the programme beneficiaries have with the programme. In the case of the NECT, ownership was created from stakeholder participation in the programme design, implementation and monitoring stages.
4. Stakeholder *participation* entails the involvement of actor groups and beneficiaries in design and implementation activities. Stakeholders carry out the implementation of programme activities and participate in decision-making about those activities. In the NECT, participation and

ownership were sought from officials responsible for the roll-out of the programmes. These officials were drawn from the provincial and district officials, teachers and their associations.

5. Programme *credibility or trustworthiness* was sought from research, evaluations and the involvement of academic experts in the design of the programmes. Independence in research and evaluations and the methodologies employed served as the basis for the integrity of the programme activities that were implemented.

6. The last MSN management fundamental is *influence*. As argued in the conceptual framework, actor groups always look for opportunities to exercise power and influence in the network. Effective leaders need to achieve network centrality, define their areas of influence and span structural holes.[81] Notably, the secretariat was observed in the NECT case study to be as interested in influence as the actor groups were. Whilst the secretariat was established with the primary purpose of managing the network, for it to achieve its goals and sustain itself, it also vied for a position of salience and built power to influence decisions in the network.

Tier 3: Management strategies and practices

The third tier of the MSN mini-model captures the management tools and practices that were observed to be critical in managing the network dynamics (Tier 1) and the MS management fundamentals (Tier 2). Two sets of strategies and practices make up Tier 3: (1) human resource management strategies and practices; and (2) systems and structures.

Human resources strategies and practices

The human resource strategies and practices comprise management practices, leadership practices, and values and principles for managing networks.

Network management practices: Management practices direct, coordinate and monitor organisational ability, individual willingness and available resources in line with the strategy.[82] These factors were found to be central to how the NECT secretariat responded to the organisational dynamics and management fundamentals making up Tiers 1 and 2 of the mini-model. Four critical network management variables discerned from the NECT case study are discussed below.

1. *Managing for network salient positioning* which has to do with how the secretariat maintained a central or salient position in the MSN, giving it agency in and leverage over the MSN. Its salient position provided the secretariat with the authority to play a central role in coordinating network activities and maintaining programme equilibrium. Salient positioning and the related agency and leverage conferred are arguably critical to securing the MSA management fundamentals such as programme legitimacy, credibility, approvals and participation, and is undoubtedly a key to MSN influence, which is necessary for the coordination of network activities.

2. *Perception management* is an ongoing risk management action aimed at eliminating the negative brand image of the network. For instance, the secretariat took conscious steps to dispel perceptions that it was dismissive of the funder actor group's design ideas, that programme implementation was moving too fast, and that the funder actor group enjoyed an unfair competitive advantage over NGOs. Communication and dialogue initiatives targeting the education sector broadly and actor groups specifically were used to address negative perceptions that emerged from time to time.

3. *Vigilant management* implies the efficiency, proactiveness and relevance with which the secretariat responded to the demands from the parent organisations. This approach includes practices that promote process efficiencies, effective communication, alertness and firmness in managing the expectations of the actor groups. In other organisational

management circumstances, vigilant management has been used as a risk management approach that promotes 'observation, detection and interpretation of weak signals and alerts'.[83] It is a strategic and tactical process that involves several people in an organisation and is used to contribute toward organisational stability and avoid crises and accidents.

4. *Staff capability* comprises several aspects that enable the secretariat to successfully manage the operations of the technical structure. Staff capability has to do with the organisation's ability to marshal, develop, direct and control financial, human, physical and information resources towards the attainment of organisational outcomes. Staff capabilities are part of the source of the secretariat's power in the structure. The critical technical staff capabilities relevant to the NECT secretariat in this regard included competent subject knowledge in the education sector and technical and tactical skills to manage large-scale MSA operations. Subject knowledge in the education sector included knowledge of the relevant policies, theories and operations of the sector. Monitoring and evaluation skills and stakeholder management skills and tactics make up other technical skills required to manage the MSN.

Network leadership practices: Leadership is authority to act, a legitimation of the right to manage and the capabilities to exercise management. The empirical data in the case study demonstrated the importance of the secretariat's leadership being recognised by the actor groups. The recognised leadership created the authority for the secretariat staff to exercise their responsibilities beyond the immediate organisational confines of the secretariat, for example, into the state and teacher union actor groups, where the secretariat staff secured recognisable accountability from over 1,000 officials who were marshalled to implement NECT programmes. Perri et al. hold the view that such accountability, which emanates from the moderately stable pattern of ties or links, is characteristic of network organisations.[84]

The same form of recognised accountability extending beyond the secretariat was used as the basis of the negotiations involving funders and teacher unions. The negotiation-oriented leadership practices adopted by the NECT entailed consultations and conflict management among actor groups, and between actor groups and the secretariat. These practices are consistent with the notion of network organisation leadership that uses persuasion and aims to cultivate loyalty, appeal to the emotions and enable the binding in of people through ceremonial events and the stylisation of those roles.[85] It emerged in the analysis that the NECT staff thought that the secretariat CEO had facilitated common visioning among actor groups, engaged in 'trust building' and created a 'sense of family' with the funders to legitimate the secretariat staff so that they could manage the network activities. The actor groups expressed an expectation of leadership that is defined by its ability to build relationships, mediate, build confidence and be exemplary.

Similarly, the secretariat adopted an organisational form defined by the concept of enclave. According to Perri et al., enclaves resort to charismatic strategies to secure network salience that is, however, fragile.[86] Such an organisational structure would use more persuasive instruments of power such as suasion, which uses information and appeals to norms, values, arguments, ideas, identification, traditions, standards and expertise, and survival instead of control and inducement, which are more forceful.

Overall, managing network organisations requires intelligent, continual 'championing, catalysing, persuasion' in order to gain, legitimate and maintain power and authority beyond the secretariat's immediate organisational sphere in which the secretariat's managers have normal employment or governance authority.

Network management principles and values: Principles and values are at the centre of organisational performance. While early management theories were concerned about the organisation and efficiencies of work, modern management theories focus more on the human factor. Values, described as 'beliefs, motivational constructs, which transcend specific actions and situations, guide selection or evaluation of actions, policies, people and events and are ordered in their importance', are part of the human factor.[87] Principles and values form the foundation of organisational behaviour and identity.

Some unique organisational principles and values that were discerned from the NECT case study are discussed below:

- Expectations to relax barriers to engagement among actor groups: For example, the teacher unions particularly emphasised the need to pay attention to engagement principles that promote 'debate' and 'depersonalisation of engagement'. The funder actor group suggested 'accommodative' engagement principles and openness to each other. Actor groups regarded formal, rigid engagements among themselves as untenable, and thus proposed flexible forms of engagement that reduce 'engagement friction' among actor groups, allowing for freer flow and competition of ideas.
- Openness and transparency expected to be values of the NECT secretariat: The funder actor group extended the expectation of openness to the other actor groups and equated openness to the willingness of actor groups 'to show their vulnerable sides'. To some extent, the principle of open engagement was demonstrated by the secretariat in the way it dealt with the teacher unions that rejected the Learning Programmes. In this regard, the secretariat used research-based evidence and dialogue to address misconceptions about the Learning Programmes and conflicts of interests among the actor groups.
- Sensitivity to politics: Actor groups had an expectation that the secretariat would be aware of the actor group positioning in respect to policies, ideologies and relationships within and between actor groups. The secretariat was expected to be capable of managing politics and to appreciate the partner organisational dynamics. Managing politics was explained

by a civil society representative as including avoidance of the internal politics of the unions and of hiring high ego and opinionated senior staff. The unique management requirements when dealing with teacher unions, as discussed above, demonstrate the need for the secretariat to watch for and anticipate the partner organisations' internal dynamics.

- The sense of joint ownership of projects: Another way that the NECT secretariat maintained actor group interest in the NECT network was to use the concept of 'joint projects'. This phrase altered the network positioning of the actor groups in specific projects. The new positioning rearranged and equalised the authority and power of the actor groups and so the actor groups saw themselves as equals.

Systems and structures

Integration and coordination mechanisms are central to networks driven through secretariats. Integration is concerned with 'achieving unity of effort among the various sub-systems in the accomplishment of the organisation's task'.[88] Integration signifies coordination, cohesion and synergy between different units.

To achieve and maintain integration, to flexibly coordinate organisations outside its direct control, and to manage and adapt to the continuous contestations in the network, the NECT secretariat adopted a flexible, non-hierarchical organisational structure.

In the NECT case study, monitoring and evaluation systems, network-wide reporting systems and oversight committees were employed to manage the network dynamics. These structures included, for instance, joint oversight structures such as project teams that saw to the establishment of the Learning Programmes, task teams that investigated the unions' concerns about the Learning Programmes in Bohlabela, and the District Steering Committees that oversaw the implementation of the NECT programmes in districts. Communication mechanisms such as annual reports, output-to-purpose reports, independently produced every two years or so, and frequent dialogues and seminars were used as sub-systems that kept the members of the NECT network regularly informed and engaged.

The structures and the systems of the NECT drew from various management schools of thought. For instance, the phenomenon of oversight committees is consistent with the management approaches that value community and political freedoms; the monitoring and evaluation systems gravitate towards the approaches that primarily centre around beliefs in order and material freedom, efficiency through planning and evidence-based planning and making use of technical approaches. Key to setting up the systems of structures of the secretariat was taking a pragmatic approach that drew from several management philosophies and aligned the configuration of the secretariat to the management requirements making up Tiers 1 and 2 of the mini-model. Managing network organisations requires unique human resource capabilities, systems and structures configured to manage complex multiple interests against the common goals of actor groups.

Observables

This chapter used the experiences in the NECT network to model how education collaborations can be managed. In the case of the NECT, two aspects were identified to be core in the management of collaborations: managing for sustainability (contractual management) and managing for programme impact (programme management).

1. Contractual management of MSNs revolves around the influence of the mother organisations (funders and founders) on the operations of the secretariat (the technical structure). Too much control of the technical structure can lead to strategy drift and the stifling of innovation.
2. Programme management requires dedicated capabilities to manage dynamics in the following three categories: technical, organisational and visioning. In addition, education

programmes require the management of the following six forms of programme implementation imperatives to ensure success: approvals, legitimation, ownership, participation, credibility and influence.

A combination of human resource and systems management strategies and tactics are key to managing the programme implementation dynamics and imperatives cited above. Human resource management entails management and leadership practices and values that are unique to large-scale network programme implementation, and systems, and structure management that is non-hierarchical and uses suasion instead of coercion to achieve outcomes.

History, values and social capital create social frameworks that encourage the establishment of network organisations (collaborations) and influence how the actor groups behave in the network. The complex and dynamic interactions between actor groups produce continual change in the power and positioning of actor groups in the network. These continuous changes have to be managed by the secretariat.

5.

Roles and Operationalisation of the Multiple Stakeholder Approach

Some Nuts and Bolts of Operationalising the Multiple Stakeholder Approach

T his chapter uses the discussions and observations in the earlier sections to transcend the conceptual realm into practice. It does so by answering two questions relating to whether the MSA should be replicated and how this can be done. The obvious answer is that it should be replicated and that the best way to show how is through modelling its initiation and operationalisation.

Why multiple stakeholder organisations should be replicated

A well thought-through interface between the state and other society groupings in the development space is necessary. The structuring of this relationship needs to extend beyond development theories as we know them. New development approaches require the deliberate mining of indigenous insights and utilising these more strategically alongside other approaches. Greater collaboration between state and non-state entities is inevitable, more so given that the line between the state and civil society is becoming more blurred, power is centralised in multiple power points, a wide range of actors (state and non-state) is involved in doing the work of the state, and the state extends beyond the realm of 'bureaucrats, policies, and institutions [to include] imageries, symbols and discourses'[89] society holds about the state.

The extension of the state into – and its interface with civil society – requires approaches that go beyond the monological perception of the state in a dominant relationship to civil society.

The MSA is one approach that goes beyond concepts such as the developmental state which are based on the centrality of the state. The MSA goes beyond the polarised views that are locked into state or not-state development. Rather, the MSA promotes polycentrism which is characterised by multi-directional networking of players in society. It ushers in new ways of approaching development, where the emphasis shifts from government to governance, and where networks can address the shortcomings of the bureaucracy and the market.

The MSA holds the potential for improving the governance and the operational efficiency of education systems. It is an effective way of mobilising a wide range of tangible and intangible resources required for service delivery improvement, and can also serve as the basis for harmonising actor groups' visions for development, education systems included. Education systems can do more with additional tangible resources such as finances and material inputs, and intangible resources such as political support and labour peace, which can be achieved through effective use of the MSA.

Just like the Japanese Kaizen approach, the widely practiced MSA, which has been repeatedly used in South Africa for the past 60 years, should be elevated to a science. Significant resources have been invested through this approach, and the potential it carries warrants the systematisation of its practice. It is for this reason that I concluded my research on the subject with a model consolidating proposals about how to operationalise the MSA.

Modelling the operationalisation of the multiple stakeholder approach

Simply expressed, a model is a representation of reality, just as a model of the heart represents the organ that pumps blood in an animal. In science, models can be quantitative or qualitative. In this case, the NECT is used as the 'referent' from which the model is constructed. The 'referent' is a part of the reality represented by a model which cannot be revealed but at the expense of time, cost and danger.[90] So, instead of studying the NECT again or any other such organisation to figure out how the MSA works, I proceed to present a model of MSA.

The MSA model is outlined schematically in Figure 7. It is made up of three zones that provide some illumination on the formation of MSNs, how the actor groups engage in MSNs, and how MSNs are managed. It is a consolidation of the chronicles of collaboration, the mini-models on the formation, engagement dynamics and management of network organisations that are presented in the earlier sections as well as an extensive body of knowledge on networks, social capital, state theory, organisational theory, teacher unions, civil society organisations and private sector funding in development.

Included are sociological frames that I developed during my more than 30-year engagement with education policy and programmes and close to 16 years of serving as chief executive officer of two organisations with characteristics of the MSA.

The model purports that societal dynamics (Zone A), determine the grounds for the formation of MSNs and the values on the basis of which actor groups engage, that is, the engagement dynamics of MSNs (Zone B). Further, the model purports that the configuration of the secretariat and how it manages the network (Zone C) is in response to the network engagement dynamics that emerge from Zone B. The secretariat's operations also have an ongoing effect on the network engagements, given that the secretariat is also an actor in the network.

Figure 7: MSA formation and operationalisation model

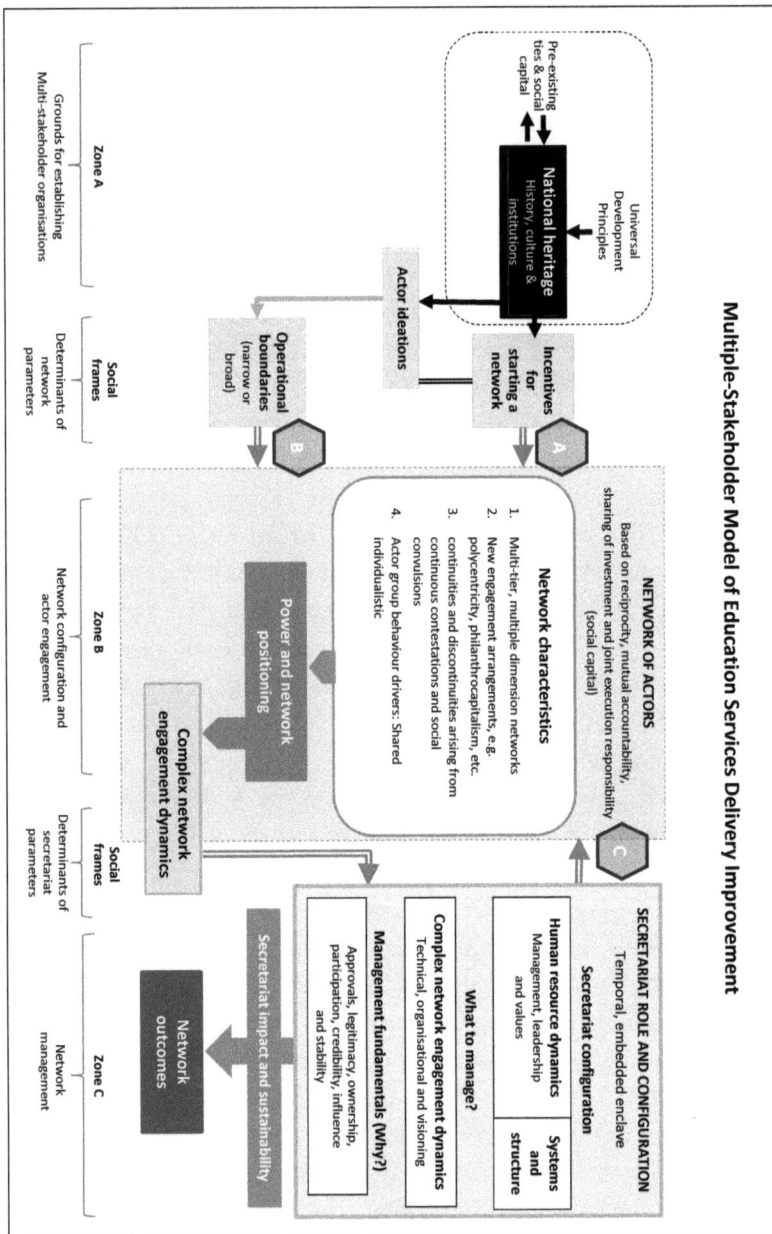

The three zones, as well as the concepts and constructs covered in the zones, are discussed further in the sections below.

Grounds for the establishment of multiple stakeholder organisations (Zone A)

The model purports that *national heritage* and *universal development principles* are the basis on which people and organisations establish MSNs. National heritage, which comprises an ensemble of recognised latent and actual societal experiences, encompasses pre-existing social ties and capital that encourage people and organisations to use the MSA.

Universal development principles emerged in the NECT case study as a set of development considerations that are not necessarily limited to or uniquely linked to the South African heritage. These included macro-development objectives espoused in the NDP, general governance improvement objectives such as the improvement of collaboration and the eradication of corruption, and promotion of educational outcomes.

Societal dynamics encompassed in Zone A create actor ideations and social frames through which histories, cultures and concepts are mediated into actor engagement patterns and network management configurations. Actor ideations entail organisational archetypes and identities linked to the organisations' reasons for existence and are the basis on which the actors decide whether to join the network. They then further inform actor engagements.

Discussing framing in the context of social movements, Gamson likens the concept to a 'building frame' which 'provides coherence to an array of symbols, images and arguments linking them through an underlying organising idea that suggests what is essential – what consequences and values are at stake'.[91] Social frames, in the context of the MS model, are conceived to include actor ideations and network operational boundaries.

The effect of the social frames on the network engagement and secretariat role is represented in the model by flowline A.

The network configuration and actor engagement sphere (Zone B)

Zone B is the sphere where the actors connect and interact to form a defined but boundaryless multi-layered and multi-dimensional network.

The construct of network includes the concept of social capital, which is about the value derived from relationships that are built on the principles of reciprocity, mutual accountability and the sharing of investment and joint execution of responsibilities. Informed by Social Frame 1, various network configurations are formed displaying patterns of connections, the 'flows', which vary in nature, the directions of interactions and the positioning of actor groups.

Much of the patterns of relationships and positioning are dependent on the actor group's resources and power. As discussed in earlier sections, actors and actor groups engage with each other based on the universal and non-universal actor group drivers (or interests). The continuous engagements of the actor groups involve ongoing contestations for power and salient positions in the network. The contestations result in continuous changes in the nature of relationships among the actors. Therefore, in Zone B, the actor groups always use their power to close structural holes and occupy salient positions, thus continually adjusting the network patterns. It is the dynamic changes in the relationships and their impact on the network that the secretariat manages continually.

The network management sphere (Zone C)

The NECT case study demonstrated that the continuous change in power and network positions result in complex actor group engagements which keep the network's engagements in a state of flux. The complex and dynamic actor group's engagements, the continuous changes in power and positions, and the importance of keeping the network programmes stable and focused (in states of equilibrium) determine the requirements and parameters of the secretariat's configuration and operations.

The network secretariat configuration is characterised by its temporal nature and embeddedness in the parent organisations (actor groups). In this regard, the actor groups with more power and leverage have more influence on the goals and the agency of the secretariat. In the model, the effects of the actor groups are transmitted to the secretariat (and the network) through flow lines A and B.

Since the secretariat is an actor in the network, that is, it exercises power and influence, it also influences the social frames through a reverse flow as in flowline A. Flowline C represents the reverse influence that the secretariat has on the actor engagements.

The key variables in the secretariat configuration are its human resources and systems and structures. The secretariat adjusts these variables to manage the complex network engagement dynamics and the resultant management fundamentals, based on flowlines A and B.

The *human resources construct* captures two elements, namely: (1) management, made up of capabilities to manage the technical structure; and (2) leadership, made up of capabilities that are able to create the authority for management to act in the context of fragile salience.

Systems and structures are means through which the secretariat ensures integration, coordination, cohesion and synergies between different actor groups. Monitoring and evaluation systems, reporting systems and oversight committees are used by the NECT secretariat to achieve unity of purpose and efforts.

The model categorises the aspects managed by the secretariat into technical, organisational and visioning aspects (as discussed in earlier sections). Also considered in the configuration of the secretariat are the network management fundamentals which the secretariat arguably has to be able to manage continuously: programme approvals, legitimation, ownership, participation, credibility and influence.

According to the model, national heritage forms the basis of social frames that influence the establishment of MSNs and the behaviours of actor groups in MSNs. In turn, the engagements of the actor groups in the network reproduce power and network positioning patterns and create new sets of dynamic social frames that determine how the secretariat manages the network.

Observables

Greater collaboration of state and non-state entities is inevitable, and robust models and frameworks that guide the engagement are necessary.

The extension of the state and its interface with business, government and civil society should embrace an approach that goes beyond monological perceptions of the actor groups to one that sees opportunities in the dynamic interaction among the actor groups.

The MSA holds the potential for improving the governance and the operational efficiency of education systems by mobilising a wide range of tangible and intangible resources required for service delivery improvement and serving as the basis for harmonising actor groups' visions for development.

Social capital embedded in societies can be harnessed to establish MSAs, influence the behaviours of actor groups in MSNs, and ensure constructive targeting and reproduction of power and network positioning patterns in development spaces.

6.

Conclusion
An Imperative to Use Networks to Respond to Market and Bureaucratic Failures

I have recounted, recorded and discussed the chronicles of collaboration in South Africa: the motivations for their establishment; the current state and how they can be better managed through secretariats or a technical structure; and whether they should and how they can be replicated. My main theory is that the MSA is a national heritage that needs to be exploited in a more deliberate and structured manner to the same extent that Kaizen is practiced in Japan, and the *ubuntu,* humanism and negritude are practiced elsewhere.

The secondary challenge is, of course, how to develop a philosophy into practical tools and instruments that can be used in organisations. The translation of philosophical approaches should be part of the bigger Africanisation project. So far, in South Africa, the MSA has delivered political emancipation and the improvement of public services through initiatives such as NEDLAC, SANAC and the NECT. The approach should be used on the basis of rigorous scholarship.

The MSA is an approach fit to be used to drive macro-development plans and to address development challenges that cannot be tackled solely through hierarchical, bureaucratic mechanisms or pure commercial PPPs. The MSA is a way of thinking that needs to be replicated in a more deliberate manner through research, policy, training and resourcing decisions.

In education, the MSA should be used as part of the search for education quality improvement solutions that have to do with the politics and governance of education. The approach holds the potential for improving the governance and the operational efficiency of education systems. It is an effective way of mobilising a wide range of tangible and intangible resources required for education improvement, and can also serve as the basis for harmonising actor groups' visions of education improvement. Education systems could do with additional tangible resources such as finances and material inputs and intangible resources such as political support and labour peace, which can be achieved through effective use of the MSA.

Greater involvement of non-state actors in the improvement of education is advocated by international development agencies such as the World Bank, the World Economic Forum, the United Nations Children's Fund, the United States Agency for International Development and the Foreign, Commonwealth & Development Office (formerly the Department for International Development). A better understanding of the identities and engagement dynamics of the state and non-state actors, explored in the earlier sections of the book, has the potential to increase the efficiencies and impact of transnational partnership initiatives such as the Global Education Partnership which seek to harness the material and non-material resources of donors and developing country governments, multilateral organisations, civil society, private companies and foundations dedicated to increasing access to quality education worldwide.

The understanding presented in this book can also be used to build guiding frameworks for private philanthropies that collaborate with governments and other non-state actors. Both the old philanthropic organisations (such as the Kellogg Foundation founded in 1930, and the Ford Foundation founded in 1936) and the new ones (such as the Bill & Melinda Gates Foundation founded in 2000 and the Mohammed Bin Rashid Al Maktoum Foundation founded in 2007)[92] that contribute trillions of dollars to development initiatives could use the lessons from this study to create new actor-group engagement approaches and funding discourses. For instance, the book highlights the implications of the implementation environments created – which can stifle or promote innovation. It further suggests that secretariats should enjoy salient network positioning and a correct mix of subject and programme management expertise to ensure that programme design and implementation are kept stable amidst continuing tensions resulting from the participation of multiple stakeholders with varied identities and interests.

While the participation of non-state entities can assist the improvement of the quality of public education services, if ill-conceived, poorly planned or poorly executed, the well-intentioned participation of non-state actor groups in public education improvement can fail to achieve the good intentions or even distract the education systems from effectively discharging their mandates. All the more reasons why we need a good conceptual and operational understanding of the MSA.

Notes

1   Joint Education Trust (2001). *Education Pathfinders: The Short Story of JET Education Services*. Joint Education Trust.
2   Banks, J.A. (1998). The lives and values of researchers: Implications for educating citizens in a multicultural society. *Education Researcher*, 27(7): 4–17.
3   McGregor, J., Nokis, L., Newberry, E., Mahdabee, L., Owl, W. and Pitwanikwat, V. (1978). Education and Elders Conference 2.
4   Clark, G.M. (1974). Career education for the mildly handicapped. *Focus on Exceptional Children*, 5(9): 1–12.
5   Khosa, G. (2023). Modelling Multiple Stakeholder Approach to Education Services Improvement: A Case Study of the National Education Collaboration Trust in South Africa. PhD thesis, University of Sussex (p. 28).
6   Suttner, R. (2006). Talking to the ancestors: national heritage, the Freedom Charter and nation-building in South Africa in 2005. *Development Southern Africa*, 23(1): 3–27.
7   World Bank (1997). *Fostering Sustainable Development: Sector Investment Programme*. World Bank.
8   Volmink, J. and Van der Elst, L. (2017). The Evolving Role of 21st Century Education NGOs in South Africa: Challenges and Opportunities. https://mietafrica.org/wp-content/uploads/2017/04/The-evolving-role-of-21st-Century-Education-NGOs-in-South-Africa.pdf
9   Statistics South Africa (StatsSA) (2012). *Census 2011: Census in Brief*. Statistics South Africa.
10 Van der Meer-Kooistra, J. and Scapens, R.W. (2015). Governing product co-development projects: The role of minimal structures. *Management Accounting Research*, 28: 68–91.
11 Suttner (2006): 3
12 Lodge, T. (1989). The United Democratic Front: Leadership and ideology. In: *Can South Africa Survive? Five Minutes to Midnight* (pp. 206–230). Palgrave Macmillan.
13 Joint Education Trust (2001).
14 African National Congress (ANC) (1994). *Reconstruction and Development Programme*.
15 ANC (1994): 8
16 Parliamentary Monitoring Group (2013). Disabled people South Africa: Briefing on education, employment and accessibility challenges.
17 National Planning Commission (NPC) (2012). *National Development Plan 2030: Our Future – Make it Work*. Office of the Precidency.
18 National Economic Development and Labour Council (NEDLAC) (1995). Discussion Document on a Framework for Social Partnership and Agreement-Making in NEDLAC.
19 NPC (2012).
20 Manuel, T. (2010). National Planning Commission: Media Briefing. http://www.thepresidency.gov.za

21 NPC (2012): 294–328.
22 NPC (2012): 314.
23 Lodge (1989): 206.
24 March, J.G. and Simon, H.A. (1965). Les organisations. Problèmes psycho-sociologiques. *Revue Française de Sociologie*, 6(1): 111.
25 Khosa (2023).
26 Department of Basic Education (DBE) (2019). 2018 National Senior Certificate Results. Department of Basic Education.
27 Howie, S.J., Combrinck, C., Roux, K., Tshele, M., Mokoena, G. and McLeod Palane, N. (2017). PIRLS Literacy 2016: Progress in international reading literacy study (PIRLS) 2016: South African children's reading literacy achievement. Centre for Evaluation and Assessment.
28 NPC (2012): 294.
29 Motshekga, A.M. (2015). Basic Education Budget Vote Speech for the 2015/16 Financial Year delivered by the Minister of Basic Education at the National Assembly in Cape Town on 06 May 2015. https://www.gov.za/speeches/asic-education-budget-vote-speech-201516-financial-year-delivered-minister-basic-education
30 Business Roundtable Statement (2019). https://www.businessroundtable.org/purposeanniversary
31 NPC (2012): 61.
32 NPC (2012): 113.
33 The Republic of South Africa (1996). *Constitution of the Republic of South Africa*. Government Printers
34 National Education Collaboration Trust (NECT) (2013). *Education Collaboration Framework: Business, Labour and Civil Society Initiative to Support the National Development Plan and the Education Sector Plan*. NECT. p. 2.
35 Graeff, P. (2009). Social capital: The dark side. In G.T. Svendsen, G.T. and G.L.H. Svendsen (Eds), *Handbook of Social Capital* (pp. 143–161). Edward Elgar.
36 Philanthro-capitalism expresses a view about how business, NGOs and, increasingly, government believe that business models and methods can produce not only economic wealth but also social welfare and social value that can enhance the public good. The contention in philanthro-capitalism is the superiority of the business sector (Gainer, B. in Taylor, R. [2010]. *Third Sector Research*. Springer).
37 Volmink and Van der Elst (2019): 13.
38 Borgatti, S.P. and Halgin, D.S. (2011). Network theorizing. *Organization Science*, 22(5): 1168–1181.
39 Hagmann, T. and Péclard, D. (2010). Negotiating statehood: Dynamics of power and domination in Africa. *Development and Change*, 41(4): 539–562.
40 Gainer, B. in Taylor, R. (2010).
41 Glaeser, E. L. (2001). The formation of social capital. *Canadian Journal of Policy Research,* 2(1): 34–40
42 Stinchcombe, A.L. (1965). Social structure and organizations. In J. March (Ed.), *Handbook of Organisations* (pp. 142–191). Rand McNally.
43 NPC (2012): 24.
44 Putman, R. (1993). *Making Democracy Work: Civic Traditions in Modern Italy*. Princeton University Press.
45 Stolle, D. and Rothstein, B. (2008). The state and social capital: An institutional theory of generalized trust. *Comparative Politics*, 40 (4): 441–459.
46 Glaeser (2001).

47   Bird, K. and Jones, K. (2000) 'Partnership' as strategy: Public–private relations in education action zones. *British Educational Research Journal*, 26(4).

48   Ibid.

49   Ginsburg, M. (2012). Public-private partnerships and the global reform of education in less wealthy countries: A moderated discussion. *Comparative Education Review*, 56 (1): 155–175.

50   United Nations Educational, Scientific and Cultural Organization (Unesco) (2007). *Education Sector-Wide Approaches (SWAps): Background, Guide and Lessons.* https://unesdoc.unesco.org/ark:/48223/pf0000150965

51   Butcher, T. (1995).

52   Ibid.: 136.

53   Halpern, D. (2005). *Social Capital*. Polity.

54   Halpern (2005).

55   Latour, B. (1996). On actor-network theory: A few clarifications. *Soziale Welt*, 47: 370.

56   Pachauri, A. (2012). Multi-stakeholder partnerships under the rajasthan education initiative: if not for profit, then for what? University of Sussex.

57   Tymon, W.G. and Stumpf, S.A. (2003). Social capital in the success of knowledge workers. *Career Development International*, 8(1): 12–20. https://doi.org/10.1108/13620430310459478

58   See Ginsburg (2012): 495.

59   Perri, P., Goodwin, N., Peck, E. and Freeman, T. (2016). *Managing Networks of Twenty-First Century Organisations*. Springer. p. 136.

60   Porter, M.E. and Kramer, M.R. (2006). The link between competitive advantage and corporate social responsibility. *Harvard Business Review*, 84(12): 78-92.

61   Péclard, D. (2010). Book review: The Contribution of Evangelical Churches to Democracy in Africa: Evangelical Christianity and Democracy in Africa. Edited by Terence O. Ranger. Oxford University Press. *The Journal of African History*, 51(1): 105–106. doi:10.1017/S0021853710000071

62   Weiner, L. (2015). Democracy, critical education, and teachers unions: Connections and contradictions in the neoliberal epoch. *Journal for Critical Education Policy Studies*, 13(2), 227–245.

63   Gainer (2010).

64   Bird (2000).

65   Bird (2000): 492.

66   Ibid.

67   Hagmann and Peclard (2010).

68   Ahmad, Y. (2006). The scope and definitions of heritage: From tangible to intangible. *International Journal of Heritage Studies*, 12(3): 292–300.

69   Blakeley, G. (2002). Civil society. In G. Blakeley and V. Bryson (Eds), *Contemporary Political Concepts: A Critical Introduction*. Pluto.

70   Perri et al. (2016): 5

71   Jessop (1998) in Ginsburg (2012).

72   Ginsburg (2012): 495.

73   Perri et al., (2016): 122.

74   Sergeeva, N. and Roehrich, J.K. (2018). Temporary multi-organizations: Constructing identities to realize performance improvements. *Industrial Marketing Management*, 75: 184–192. https://doi.org/10.1016/j.indmarman.2018.05.007

75   See Videc et al. in Perri et al. (2016): 125.

76   Perri et al. (2016): 125.

77   Meer-Kooistra (2015).

78   Perri et al. (2016): 73.
79   Abdul-Quader, A.S., Heckathorn, D.D., Sabin, K. and Saidel, T. (2006). Implementation and analysis of respondent driven sampling: Lessons learned from the field. *Journal of Urban Health*, 83: 1–5.
80   Senge, P. (1990). *The Fifth Discipline*. Doubleyday. p. 206.
81   Burt, R.S. (2002). The social capital of structural holes. In F. Mauro, R.G. Guillen, E. Paula and M. Marshall (Eds), *The New Economic Sociology: Developments in an Emerging Field* (pp. 201–247). Russell Sage Foundation.
82   Eccles, R.G., Nohria, N., Berkley, I.D. (1992). *Beyond the Hype: Rediscovering the Essence of Management*. Harvard Business School Press.
83   Brizon, A. and Wybo, J.L. (2006). Vigilance: a process contributing to the resilience of organizations. In: Rigaud, E. and Hollnagel, E. (Eds.), *Proceedings of the Second Resilience Engineering Symposium* (pp. 46–52). Presses des Mines.
84   Perri et al. (2016): 5.
85   Ibid.: 152.
86   Ibid: 125.
87   James, P.S. (2014). Aligning and propagating organizational values. *Procedia Economics and Finance*, 11: 95–109.
88   Khosa (2023): 147.
89   Ibid.: 61.
90   Schut, C. and Bredeweg, B. (1996). An overview of approaches to qualitative model construction. *The Knowledge Engineering Review*, 11(1): 1–25.
91   Gamson, C.R. (2015). Are frames enough? In J.G. Japser (Ed.), *Social Movements Reader: Cases and Concepts* (pp. 136–142). Wiley Blackwell.
92   See https://www.therichest.com/the-biggest/10-biggest-philanthropy-foundations-worldwide/

About the Author

Godwin Khosa is the founding CEO of the National Education Collaboration Trust (NECT). He served as CEO of JET Education Services for nearly five years before his appointment at the NECT. While at JET Education Services he headed the NECT Secretariat pending the establishment of the Trust's full-time office.

A teacher by profession, Dr Khosa worked as a policy analyst and senior manager at the Centre for Education Policy Development in the 1990s before joining the Human Sciences Research Council (HSRC) as a research manager and proceeding to JET Education Services. There he served initially as a team leader on an education transformation programme in Limpopo and then as the organisation's Programme Director before being appointed CEO in 2009. Dr Khosa has served on various committees, including as member of Council of the University of Johannesburg from 2012 to 2021.

He holds a doctoral degree from the University of Sussex; a diploma and a master's degree in Public and Development Management from the University of Witwatersrand; a BA (Hons) in Geography from the University of South Africa, and a BA in Education from the University of the North.

www.ingramcontent.com/pod-product-compliance
Lightning Source LLC
Chambersburg PA
CBHW040149270326
41929CB00025B/3436